ADVANCE PRAISE FOR *TOUCH*

"It's been over a decade since social media changed the way that businesses connect with their consumers and their employees. So, where are we at? In *TOUCH*, Mark Blevis and Tod Maffin argue that even though technology has enabled us to connect like never before, we've actually moved in the opposite direction. We have removed the real and human connections. It's time to bring that human touch back to business. This book lays out the perfect blueprint. Want to be more human? Start with *TOUCH*."

— **MITCH JOEL**, President, Twist Image, and author of *Six Pixels of Separation* and *CTRL ALT Delete*

"People want to do business with other people. That's been true since the beginning of time. A hundred years ago our great-grandparents knew the people who sold them hardware or shoes or chickens. But in an era of mass media, we've lost the human touch. Now it is time to regain humanity in business and Mark and Tod will show you how in this well-written and informative guide."

— **DAVID MEERMAN SCOTT**, international bestselling author of *The New Rules of Marketing & PR*

"*TOUCH* offers a refreshing look at the humanity behind our digital-centric lives, with practical tips for putting the humanity back in business. Make these TOUCHpoints your guide to the business of the future."

— **SCOTT MONTY**, Executive Vice-President of Strategy, SHIFT Communications (former Global Digital & Multimedia Communications Manager for Ford Motor Company)

"Evidence continues to mount that customers are more likely to do business with brands that behave well. From demonstrating you're serious about sustainability to every employee engaging in customer service, from producing content that genuinely helps people to finding third-party reports of great interactions with the company, mountains of research show that success increasingly depends on taking a human approach to business. Just in time, Tod Maffin and Mark Blevis have produced *TOUCH*, a concise, readable, and
sure your company has a soul. Of all the

demonstrate these days when power has shifted to the customer, humanity should be at the top of the list. Whether your organization has been hammered for its compassionless approach to business or you're just not satisfied with the degree of humanity already evident in your operations, you'll want to not just read, but use, *TOUCH*."

— **SHEL HOLTZ**, principal, Holtz Communication & Technology and author or co-author of many books, including *Tactical Transparency*

"Every now and again, a book makes you flip a LOT of your thoughts upside down and look at them from a different angle. *TOUCH* is that book. Maffin and Blevis force you into a strange world while pointing out that it's where you wanted to be all along."

— **CHRIS BROGAN**, CEO, Owner Media Group and author of several books, including *Trust Agents* and *The Freaks Shall Inherit the Earth*

"Tod and Mark are both some of the earliest pioneers of social media, and I have been watching them work for years. Heed their advice — it may make every difference for your business."

— **JULIEN SMITH**, Co-founder and CEO, Breather, and co-author of *Trust Agents* and *The Impact Equation*

"Maffin and Blevis rightfully point out that in order to succeed in today's competitive landscape, it's time to start relating to our customers and employees as human beings. They offer simple but powerful steps to help your company move towards becoming more relatable, real — and ultimately — more successful."

— **KARIN BASARABA**, International Association of Business Communicators

"Mark and Tod ask leadership to look at technology and ask 'What will it do TO me?' not 'What will it do FOR me?' Regardless of the size of enterprise you are in, technical change is constant and necessary. Tod and Mark show us in an easy-to-understand way that embracing technology correctly means understanding how it affects us on a human scale."

— **STEVE DOTTO**, Host, Dotto Tech

TOUCH

FIVE FACTORS TO
GROWING AND
LEADING A HUMAN
ORGANIZATION

TOD MAFFIN
MARK BLEVIS

DUNDURN
TORONTO

Project Editor: Carrie Gleason
Copy Editor: Natalie Meditsky
Cover design: Shane Potvin
Hand illustrations: Shane Potvin
Design: Jesse Hooper
Printer: Webcom

The image on p236 used with permission. Jack Daniel's trademarks appear courtesy of Jack Daniel's Properties, Inc. Jack Daniel's is a registered trademark of Jack Daniel's Properties, Inc.

Library and Archives Canada Cataloguing in Publication

Maffin, Tod, author
    Touch : five factors to growing and leading a human organization / Tod Maffin, Mark Blevis.

Issued in print and electronic formats.
ISBN 978-1-4597-2874-5 (pbk.).--ISBN 978-1-4597-2875-2 (pdf).--
ISBN 978-1-4597-2876-9 (epub)

    1. Information resources management. 2. Industrial relations--Effect of technological innovations on. 3. Management information systems. 4. Electronic commerce. I. Blevis, Mark, author II. Title.

T58.64.M34 2014   658.4'038   C2014-904979-X
                                         C2014-904980-3

1 2 3 4 5   18 17 16 15 14

  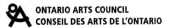

We acknowledge the support of the **Canada Council for the Arts** and the **Ontario Arts Council** for our publishing program. We also acknowledge the financial support of the **Government of Canada** through the **Canada Book Fund** and **Livres Canada Books**, and the **Government of Ontario** through the **Ontario Book Publishing Tax Credit** and the **Ontario Media Development Corporation**.

Care has been taken to trace the ownership of copyright material used in this book. The author and the publisher welcome any information enabling them to rectify any references or credits in subsequent editions.

J. Kirk Howard, President

The publisher is not responsible for websites or their content unless they are owned by the publisher.

Printed and bound in Canada.

VISIT US AT
Dundurn.com | *@dundurnpress* | *Facebook.com/dundurnpress* | *Pinterest.com/Dundurnpress*

Dundurn
3 Church Street, Suite 500
Toronto, Ontario, Canada
M5E 1M2

CONTENTS

ACKNOWLEDGEMENTS

Thanks to the great team at Dundurn Press, who led us through the process — specifically, Margaret Bryant for embracing the concept, Carrie Gleason for keeping us on track with our deadlines, Karen McMullin for her expert sales support, and Caitlyn Stewart for her assistance in early promotion of the material.

Our editor, Don Loney, provided incalculably valuable input on everything from consistency of voice to questioning the conclusions we'd arrived at. Don inspired us to be better authors.

Shane Potvin took our scattered design and turned the cover art into a piece of brilliance. Rob Cottingham lent his comedy brain for the opening chapter illustrations. And John Meadows braved cool temperatures to make us look good in photos he took outside of our hotel.

Martin Perelmuter and his amazing team at Speakers' Spotlight believed in the project from day one and provided a great sounding board to help us glean what information business leaders could use in this kind of book. Special thanks to agent Dwight Ireland, whose initial germ of an idea led to this concept.

Thank you also to the long list of business leaders and experts we interviewed as part of our research. They shared their expertise and insights with us and we're grateful for it.

Our friends (and business superstars in their own right) Mitch Joel, Scott Stratten, and Julien Smith all offered wise advice on the initial stages of finding the right publishing partner. They were also a great cheering section.

TOD'S THANKS

This whole project started when Mark and I realized, over lunch one day, that we were both separately working on roughly the same concept of this book. We joined forces and the result couldn't have been better. Mark and his wife, Andrea, have been a great support, letting me bounce ridiculous ideas off their brains. Mark didn't freak out when I (regularly) missed deadlines we both had agreed to. It's wonderful to have a great coauthor; it's even better to have that coauthor be a great friend.

My wife, Jocelyn, has been an enormous part of this project — helping research ideas, providing great input on structure, and just generally talking me down off the ledge when the stress of word counts and looming deadlines wreaked havoc on my brain. (A Post-it Note she left one morning on the printed draft manuscript reading "Work on me today! I want to grow up to be a real book one day!" was probably entirely responsible for two chapters getting done on time.)

My mom, herself a respected author, and my stepfather, Hans, both acted as quiet cheerleaders in the wings, pushing without pushing.

Special thanks needs to be paid to my assistant, Geneva Bokowski, who did much of the legwork in research, booking calls with business leaders, and coordinating the important publishing deadlines. Geneva is a force of nature and I'm lucky to have her on my team.

Martin Perelmuter and the whole team at Speakers' Spotlight is amazing to work alongside of, and special thanks need to go to Cathy Hirst and Jackie Miller for their decades-long encouragement (browbeating?) of me to write a book (usually phrased as "Hey — why haven't you written that damned book yet?!"). I'm proud to have worked with both of them on the speaking circuit for more than fifteen years now and even prouder to call them friends.

MARK'S THANKS

I consider myself very lucky to be both a friend and collaborator of Tod's. This book project has been fun and educational. Its origins, and many amazing friendships, can be traced back to a radio segment Tod did in March 2005. That's a different story. This book was conceived over lunch with Tod and his (now) wife, Jocelyn. It's a lunch I will always remember. Thank you both!

I can't imagine accomplishing even half of the things I've set out to do without the support of my wife, Andrea. Andrea has always been a positive and practical supporter of all of my projects, no matter how crazy they are. She's more than a partner to me. I can't imagine life without her.

Just as Andrea has been a positive and practical supporter, our daughters, Lucy and Bayla, have been (and continue to be) amazingly patient with me. I always have a million things on the go. If it's not work, it's the book. If it's not the book, it's a research project. And so on. I'm grateful for them.

My aunt Myrna has been encouraging me to write a book for years. She's been one of my life cheerleaders for as long as I can remember, including during this project.

My team at FullDuplex — Émilie, Victoria, and Heather — have all helped research aspects of this book. They've also brought levity to the office when I've needed it most.

My FH alumni network of Michael von Herff, Eric Lamoureux, Paul Monlezun, David Kaiser, Anne Lachance, John Sparks, and the Honourable Monte Solberg have all directly or indirectly had an impact on this book. It's a privilege to work with them.

Thank you also to all of the media professionals and research collaborators who constantly test my knowledge and ideas with interesting questions.

I dedicate this book to my uncle and mentor, Ken Ain. Thank you for everything. I miss you.

CHAPTER 1

A LETTER TO YOU FROM US

Dear Leader:

First, the good news. The digital world has fundamentally changed how organizations hire staff, market their services, and connect with stakeholders and the public. It's provided cost savings and greater efficiency. And it's helped start-ups bootstrap themselves into NASDAQ-listed companies in a heartbeat.

Not without a cost.

The same technology that helped organizations overcome geographically dispersed workforces that crossed the International Date Line also drove a wedge in localized workforces. By trying to make life easier for young families and reduce facilities-costs through telecommuting, organizations instead discovered that team members being distant in the same city created a new series of complications.

Many organizations have embraced digital business tools at the expense of retaining humanity in all of their dealings. In an effort to use high tech to connect with people more effectively, we are losing the human "touch" — that critical person-to-person connection — which is still the engine of commerce.

- Hiring is done by automated keyword searches.

- Offices have regressed to sterile, highly controlled environments.

- Communications staff increasingly rely on scripted responses.

- Websites are designed for search engines, not people.

- Leaders focus on arbitrary "best practices" metrics.

This erosion of humanity in business isn't a story that's often picked up by the business media. After all, it's not sexy and it doesn't fit the narrative of advanced technology solving all business problems. It's become clear that in a world filled with complicated web forms and digital marketing services, we have lost the human element in how we run our organizations.

Here is what we offer in terms of restoring the human touch:

- **Leadership:** defining your organization's human values, speaking the business language of humanity, becoming a "Chief Humanizing Officer";

- **Customer service:** combatting the death of loyalty, fostering a new ethic in your call centres, defining the role of the "brandividual";

- **Web/social:** understanding the new human digital metrics, creating a people-based online experience, doing web workflow the right way;

- **Marketing:** identifying influencers and leading brand advocates, exploiting personal data pools, exploring next-generation human marketing;

- **Crisis communications:** responding to those with "digital personality disorder," implementing the SWARM methodology, managing your brand reputation the human way; and

- **Legal:** approaching necessary legal communications more humanely.

We believe the same telecommuting technology that had its origins in time- and place-shifting our interactions has evolved into "telecommuniting" technology that allows us to have meaningful real-time, and even time-shifted, interactions within an organization as well as with stakeholders, the media, and the public.

Our book will help you discover why and how.

Thank you for picking up a copy and reading this far. Your journey is just beginning.

Sincerely,

Tod and Mark
@todmaffin
@markblevis

CHAPTER 2
THE FIVE FACTORS

Infusing your organization with more humanity isn't as simple as following a recipe. There's no easy step-by-step solution that you can implement. Rather, increasing what we call the TOUCH factor in all areas of your operations is an evolving process, measured with softer metrics than some leaders are comfortable with. After all, KPI (key performance indicators) dashboards don't often measure the soft stuff.

Based on our own experiences and conversations with countless business and community leaders, we've identified five overall factors which are key to growing and leading a human-based organization. As you'll see, they're not tactical steps to check off a list. Rather, they're an overall ethos that must become a part of your organizational commitment to human values.

We'll spend just a bit of time on these five factors, then spend the rest of the book discussing how you can instill these values in all aspects of your organization.

TECHNOLOGY

It might seem counterintuitive to put technology at the top of the list of factors necessary to humanize your organization. The fact is, technology can be your strongest ally. There are thousands of web services, software as a service (SaaS) products, and digital tools which can help you inflect more humanity into the mix.

Let's start with some important guideposts.

Hire Your Technology

Stop thinking about your technology as nothing more than a computer. You should treat your business technology as you would an actual human employee. Have a job description for which a technological solution may apply. Then, conduct regular performance reviews (luckily, your technology won't ask for a pension).

- Does the technology that serves your organization still do as good a job now as when you first brought it on board?

- Is it taking too many sick days (downtime)?

- Do you have a growth and succession plan in place for when you exceed its capabilities?

In far too many cases, the answer to these questions is either "No" or "I have no idea."

We're not talking about a general sense of these items either. Schedule annual performance reviews of your CRM (customer relationship management) system. Invite the people who work closest with it. Ask them to submit reviews of the system's job performance over the past year. Ask these colleagues of the technology to advise on when it needs to be promoted (more money invested in it) or fired.

This regular performance review (call it a "tech audit" if you're uncomfortable with the human language) is critical because your business grows, your stakeholders change over time, and your objectives shift. Your business technology should evolve with these changes.

Work Backwards

The first technology decisions that contribute to the dehumanizing of organizations often come from forcing your people or customers to adapt to your technology and not the other way around.

You've probably been on the receiving end of this. At one time you and your outsourced designer were just fine sending emails back and forth. In an effort to achieve greater efficiency, she brought on a complicated project management website. Now, you have to make sure you're emailing the right Dropbox address, you're not sure which members of the team are receiving your replies, and you can't view attachments without logging into the new platform. Hell, where *did* you put that password, anyway?

To align your business technology with the humans you serve and lead, you must start with the customer or employee experience and work backwards to the technology.

Steve Jobs said it best:

> You can't start with the technology and try to figure out where you're going to try to sell it. I've made this mistake probably more than anybody in this room and I've got the scar tissue to prove it, and I know that it's the case. As we have tried to come up with a strategy and a vision for Apple, it started with 'What incredible benefits can we give to the customer? Where can we take the customer?' [It's] not starting with 'Let's sit down with the engineers and figure out what awesome technology we have and how are we going to market that?'[1]

Anticipate, Don't React

Here's one reason the robot overlords haven't seized control of Earth yet — we humans have instinct, gut feelings, and the ability to anticipate needs with greater accuracy than machines. (Though this is a close race — IBM's Jeopardy-playing robot, Watson, was able to predict when it was likely to get an answer wrong. In one question under the category "U.S. Cities," Watson guessed "Toronto?????" — complete with the five question marks. Because Watson was able to doubt the strength of the answer, the computer bet only a fraction of its money pool, prompting host Alex Trebek to shout, "Oh, you sneak!")

Remember there are many human-centric steps in any decision cycle, whether it's a purchase decision, hiring decision, or management decision. Steps like "consideration" are often ignored by technology platforms. Instead, we get marketing automation tools which merely keep bugging people until they buy something.

Some companies are working toward anticipating purchases before customers even commit to buying. A recent patent filed by Amazon reveals its plan for "anticipatory package shipping." Amazon's system identifies near-purchases (like the act of placing items in a digital cart, adding items to a wish list, or even long cursor hovers over specific items listed on its website) and begins the process of shipping based on that behaviour. Packages are sent to shipping hubs or directly to trucks in anticipation of the Purchase button being clicked. This would let Amazon ship copies of a popular book on the day it's published, for example. To reduce the number of returns, Amazon says it might offer a steep discount to deliver the product anyway or, if it's a low-cost item, provide it as a thank-you gift. It's a simple tactic, yet one which makes the company more connected to the real-world day of its customers.

On the human resources side, being able to forecast issues through surveys or by simply tracking them on a calendar can alert you to needs which are likely to arise.

In your customer service department, you should be using tools that let you monitor social chatter which may turn into issues you're forced to deal with. For larger brands, this can be as simple as monitoring mentions of your brand or product names online alongside a list of hot words like "broken," "missing," or "lousy," and popping in with a gentle "Can I be of service?" message. Follow-through is critical.

In public relations and public affairs, resources should be dedicated to monitoring public opinion online, measuring reaction to campaigns, issues, and activities. Proactive research and sentiment analysis will allow you to anticipate changes in opinion and better equip you to change course and communicate effectively before an issue takes on a life of its own — a life in which you have little or no part.

OUTCOMES

You've probably felt it before — the dread of year-end measurement against the same key performance indicators (KPIs). These indicators, like cost per acquisition, customer attrition rate, and bad debt recovery, are important to guide your organization to success.

Far too often, leaders mistakenly direct their focus on measuring hard numbers, often drowning in data without understanding how their activities impact real humans.

Breathing more humanity into these outcomes — and even providing some softer, yet measurable, metrics — will go a long way.

Why, Not What

Human organizations must articulate the sole purpose they have for existing. Reducing customer attrition may indeed be a compelling objective, but it doesn't define *why* you do what you do. Each leader should be able to articulate to their team why the organization exists in the first place.

Consider the vision of Vancity, the largest English-language credit union in Canada. It's clear: "At Vancity, our vision is to redefine wealth."

Their vision statement continues, explaining that the organization feels it needs to "re-envision prosperity as something we can only achieve if we are surrounded by and connected to a vibrant, healthy community that is sustainable for the long term."

It's a welcome change from the usual vision of outcomes like increasing shareholder value. Ask the *benefit* that humans gain from increasing shareholder value. Can they afford better things for their kids? How does it improve their day-to-day life? How will it change how they view the world?

Your first step is to understand and explain the human reasons you do something. Only then can you measure your success in that space.

Simple, Human KPIs

We need a new model of measuring success in organizations — one that understands the effect your operations have on real people.

As with each of the five factors outlined in this book, this new look at business can and should cross each of your departments.

One approach we like is business advisor and strategist Chris Brogan's annual exercise in selecting three words which guide his priorities in each upcoming year. His 2014 focus words are:

> **Lifestyle** — I'm using this to cover my fitness/health efforts, my financial health, my choices in how I spend my time. It's a big one covering much more than the word usually covers.

> **Monchu** — The network is everything. I'm committed to doing even more for the people I serve in 2014. This is a huge focus for me, my business, my speeches, my pursuits. Oh wait, maybe you don't know what the word *Monchu* means. "Monchu" is an Okinawan word that means "one family" or sometimes "extended family" or sometimes "the family we choose."

> **Black** — As in "get in the black." I don't mean my finances (though I'll be working on financial strengthening this coming year), but also my life choices, my ability to build the marketplace to achieve what I can help it accomplish. I mean to invest in my world and grow my capabilities. The general feeling when I say this word in my own head is "all is right with the world." That's the goal.

You can read more about Chris's words strategy at *http://touchthebook. com/3words*.

Chris's words centre on his personal growth.

Your organization could adopt the same approach and clarify your overall outcomes with three simple words. These act like mantras across your firm, focusing your teams on the human impact of your business. Should you decide to employ this idea, be sure you have a clear understanding of how you'll measure growth toward these word themes.

For instance, if one word is *listen*, determine metrics for ensuring your organization is picking up the subtleties of conversation around and throughout your business, using social media monitoring tools, proactive surveying, informal employee town hall meetings, and conversations — formal and informal — wherever they may occur.

Dan Heath, coauthor of several books including *Made to Stick*, demonstrates the danger of creating mission statements by committee in the FastCompany video *How to Write a Mission Statement That Doesn't Suck.*[2] In it, Dan walks through an example of a great mission statement employees can understand and get behind becoming increasingly meaningless as a committee softens word choice and each participant makes sure his or her own purpose is cemented into the corporate mission.

Former Apple evangelist Guy Kawasaki laments the amount of his life wasted in mission-setting meetings with dozens of senior leaders. He offers a compelling alternative: a mantra.

> A mantra is three or four words long. Tops. Its purpose is to help employees truly understand why the organization exists.
>
> If I were the CEO of Wendy's, I would establish a corporate mantra of "healthy fast food." End of story.

Some other examples of corporate mantras:

- **Federal Express:** "Peace of mind"

- **Nike:** "Authentic athletic performance"

- **Target:** "Democratize design"

- **Mary Kay:** "Enriching women's lives"

Dan Pontefract, author of *Flat Army: Creating a Connected and Engaged Organization* and head of the Telus department overseeing cultural change in the organization, agrees. "When you are going through an organizational change, your organization needs a mantra and I think you as an individual need one."

"At Telus, we adopted the mantra "Culture is our competitive advantage."

It must be working. In the summer of 2007, employee engagement at Telus was 53 percent. Today, it is 83 percent.

DISCLOSURE

But it's not enough to decide on and communicate these additional KPIs and ultra-short mission statements. For progress toward your organization's outcomes to be clearly understood by people in the trenches, you need to make sure evidence of progress is clear.

Vancouver digital marketing firm 6S Marketing uses computer screens in its office, displaying real-time metrics like sales targets and public social media mentions to team members. They use salesforce-based software called Hoopla, which "jazzes up" metrics as a kind of running game — including a top-sales-performer scoreboard, complete with virtual awards and a gong sound that plays when a sale is closed. (See *touchthebook.com/hoopla* for more information on how 6S uses this system.)

Of course, disclosure doesn't need to have such a highly ratcheted-up cool factor. Something as simple as an internal magazine (physical or digital) that highlights progress toward metrics can suffice. Don't limit this information to your senior executives and shareholders; sharing it with your people will help increase morale and prove that progress is being made toward clear goals.

UNIQUENESS

Too many organizations rely on the same customer service responses, the same benefits programs, and the same procedures. There's nothing wrong with studying and using best practices in your business. Still, to become a more human organization you need to stand above the crowd in all aspects of your business.

In their 1990 book *Creating the Service Culture: Strategies for Canadian Business*, authors Stanley A. Brown, Marvin B. Martenfeld, and Allan Gould suggest that, at some point, all business offerings will become essentially homogeneous. When that happens, they hypothesize success will be defined less by a product or service itself and more by the experience of the buyer and end-user. Product similarities are the subject of many a patent lawsuit these days. Like in Hollywood, where a studio's gamble on a penguin movie spawns an entire genre of penguin movies, tech titans and start-ups that launch innovative products spawn entire categories — blue oceans which quickly become bloody red waters of competition.

When innovation winds down, revenues dry up.

Perhaps this explains the emergence of companies with a mission to collect patents and protect them through lawsuits.

Product innovation takes a lot of capital investment. It takes research, development, user interface considerations, quality assurance testing, creative marketing efforts, and is subject to safety standards and other regulatory restrictions. It's a complex process. And, because these stages have been widely accepted for many years, they're largely relied upon as the proven process.

BEING UNIQUE ISN'T EXCLUSIVELY ABOUT HAVING THE MOST REMARKABLE PRODUCT. IT'S ABOUT *BEING* REMARKABLE.

The original *Star Wars* movie was acclaimed for its groundbreaking special effects. But it wasn't a blockbuster hit because director George Lucas invested heavily in developing new special effects technology to tell his story. As Danny Brown, coauthor of *Influence Marketing*, pointed out in his TEDxOttawa talk,[3] *Star Wars* was the highest-grossing film for six years because it was a human-relatable story of overcoming the odds set in gritty conditions, "a long time ago in a galaxy far away," and was released at a time when the sci-fi genre was about the pristine technology of the future. The prequel, released twenty-two years later, was a marvel of special effects technology with an extremely weak story by comparison; all tech, no TOUCH.

Being human should be natural to all of us. After all, we are human. However, we're often conditioned to suppress our emotions and present a brave, optimistic, and successful face. We're often taught failure is not an option. For some reason, apologies have become synonymous with admitting negligence (apologies are covered in more detail in the chapter about leadership).

Dealing with suffering is neither unique nor unusual. The death of a parent is unavoidable. However, we often pretend this type of reality doesn't exist. That's why the public is bowled over when politicians, CEOs, and community leaders declare their humanity by tweeting an apology for some misdeed, or publishing a blog post about the passing of a relative. Interestingly, the leaders who do this well often earn respect from the people who hear them out — supporters and critics alike.

Authenticity earns respect.

Perhaps you're the manager of a team of airline staff who proactively rebook all of the connections for passengers of a flight that is delayed arriving at its destination, or a social media manager who responds to customer service concerns with genuine surprise and apology. In real, human tones.

The important lesson here is to offer something your competition does not. And remember that your competition could just as likely be other leadership candidates within your own organization as it could be a tech titan with a superior product.

WHAT DO YOUR CUSTOMERS SAY IS YOUR UNIQUE DEFINING QUALITY? DO A SURVEY.

CLARITY

A human organization is clear. It knows how it serves its communities, how it communicates, and how it runs its business.

Every communication effort can benefit from clarity.

Consider how clarity applies to your communications department. Are you using simple language that reflects the way people really talk in your news releases, or are you relying on old "tried-and-true" phrasing like "ABC Corp is excited to announce blah blah blah"?

Clarity is one of the defining qualities of the Creative Commons.[4] Founders James Boyle, Lawrence Lessig, and Hal Abelson took the process of licensing creative works, which had become complex from years of legal interference, and made it easier for copyright holders. Creative Commons provides tools and plain language which help copyright holders decide how they would like to license their works, and how they will communicate those licences. The licences are written in a way that facilitates a clearer understanding of the conditions under which others can use those works. Parameters include whether or not attribution is required, whether or not users can make money from the use and sale of the work, and whether or not users must enforce the same licensing parameters to downstream users.

Clarity is not hard to measure. One place to start is to conduct a clarity audit on your outward-facing materials. Can people understand what you're trying to say? Like a bad joke, if it requires too much explanation to be appreciated, your message was probably not received.

End-user licence agreements (EULAs), community, and privacy policies are frequently criticized for being too long and too legal. At roughly fifty-six pages, the iTunes music store licence is unfathomably long for the average user to read, much less understand. Which is probably why so many people who use iTunes have no idea what they've agreed to (include us in that group).

The Tim Hortons coffee shop Wi-Fi terms-of-use agreement is 2,268 words long. Since the average person reads roughly 250 words per minute, the nine minutes it would take one of us to read the agreement would be longer than it would take to drink our coffee. That means most of us would be ready to leave before we were in a position to accept the terms and do anything meaningful online.

Privacy policies are another conundrum.

Tod's website privacy policy is written in clear language. And, because the "personality" of his brand is friendly and even a bit non-traditional, it reads like someone speaking:

> Man, I hate nosy browsers. I hate them worse than you do.... Still, there's that whole "balance" thing — should I strip all good functionality out of my site and make it marginally functional but butt-ugly (I'm looking at you, Craigslist) or make it a more helpful site at the expense of some cookie-collecting?
>
> I'm opting for the second.
>
> **What I Know About You:** The only information my site collects about you are things that every single other web server in the world collects — your IP address, what web page your browser requested, and some basic info about your computer (your operating system, screen resolution, etc.). All websites collect this info. All of them. In fact, there's no way to not collect this info. It's just how the Web was built.
>
> **What I Do Not Know About You:** Unless you manually fill in a form giving me that info, I have no idea who you are. I don't know your age, your phone number, your email address, your street address, or why your mom calls you "Bosso." Nothing you do on my site identifies you without you knowing about it. I mean, I suppose you could be filling in a Contact Me form in your sleep, but if that's the case, you probably have bigger problems to deal with....
>
> **Don't Blame Me:** Also, my site uses some pretty standard third-party services (like Wufoo to make forms, Google to keep track of analytics, AdRoll to present you with reminders about my site in banner ads when

you're elsewhere on the Web, and so on). All these
people have their own privacy policies, most likely
written by people far more intelligent than I. I don't
have any control of what their sites or cookies do,
but I wouldn't use them if I thought they were evil.
You should probably read their own policies if you're
freaked out about this stuff.

Of course, his light tone might not be appropriate for your brand.
Still, there's likely plenty of room for your official documents to be
made less, well, officious.

By the way, you can read Tod's entire privacy policy at *http://
todmaffin.com/privacy.*

Clarity, of course, does not imply complete organizational transparency. You don't need to publish everyone's salaries online (though at
least one company, BufferApp.com, does exactly that — and outlines the
calculation it uses to determine what it pays people).

Clarity is about simplicity in your communications and directness
in your phrasing. Legal, human resources (HR), sales, contracting,
shipping and receiving … every department in every organization will
benefit from clarity

HUMANITY

Finally, the most important factor. In all your efforts, you should strive to
inject humanity into the mix. While many organizations find it difficult
to make humanity part of their day-to-day operations, it's actually easier
than you might think — even in the digital age.

Mark has often referred to this as making "digital eye contact." That
is, being able to gain the undivided attention of an audience, no matter
how small or large, even for a moment. It is possible to make eye contact
online in a way that's analogous to making eye contact with your lunch
companion, the people you're having a coffee with, or the conference hall
you're addressing. You need to be your human self, speak in a human
tone, and use human language and human-relatable experience.

Instinct

Human companies have learned how to trust their "organizational gut feeling," as articulated by the people in the trenches. If you've hired properly, you'll have a team of smart, sensitive, feeling people. Their first instincts are often the best for your business.

For instance, consider how many organizations end up crippling their own efforts by trusting data over instinct. Suppose you issue a detailed Request for Proposal (RFP) to build a Customer Relationship Management (CRM) platform. You'll receive vendor proposals, each detailed by the requirements outlined in your RFP. But these data points don't make up the entire picture. Immeasurable factors like "I just got a funny vibe from the sales guy" are as important (if not more so) than the line items detailed in the vendors' responses.

While most organizations use the simple response-evaluating equation of Ability + Price = Decision, you should also factor intuitiveness into this calculation. Thus, decisions should be more along the lines of Ability + Price + Gut Feeling = Decision.

Back in 2000, Tod founded a dot-com company called MindfulEye, which developed artificial intelligence to understand the meaning behind online chatter. With this software, companies could gauge the subjective mood of public opinion on the Internet. With a few clicks, you could see a chart of people's opinion of a given company. Tod's company went public in eighteen months, and this category would later be known as sentiment analysis.

Several venture capital firms were vying to be the company's second-round funder. Tod and his partners met with three such firms and evaluated them based on their past performance, skills of executives, and the proposed valuation and terms. But at one of these meetings, Tod's group got a bad vibe from one of the vying firm's leaders. They couldn't put their finger on it, but something struck them as odd — perhaps a sense of distraction, perhaps of looking for a quicker stock turnaround than they wanted. Still, that group's proposal on paper seemed strongest, and they discounted their gut feelings and went with that group.

While MindfulEye did well, they later found their instincts had been right — that firm probably wasn't the best partner for long-term growth. MindfulEye grew to about twenty people before being caught up in the dot-com bomb and was unable to secure additional funding rounds. Trusting their gut would have placed the company on a more fruitful path.

Stories

Another component of building humanity into your organization's mix is using anecdotes and storytelling as part of the corporate ethos. Leaders certainly need to communicate important information to their troops, but each time you do, you should look for a human story to articulate the impact on your actual customers, employees, shareholders, and partners.

This will be easier for some departments than others. Many marketing groups already develop character portraits to represent the people in their markets. ("Jill is a thirty-year-old junior executive who loves to travel and is trying to be better at fitness.") But this kind of anecdotal information can and should extend to all parts of your organization.

- Your legal team should try to understand someone's motivation for using your brand imagery without your permission. (Perhaps they're a superfan and are trying to connect with your firm or share their enthusiasm to attract others to the products and services you offer.)

- Your human resources team should define custom benefits packages based on the real-world needs of your employees, not just accept what's offered by a benefits administration firm.

- Your customer service team should rely less on scripts and instead try to picture the way people are interacting with your product or service, to better empathize with frustrations.

The ability to relate to people and communicate that quality in stories isn't restricted to the Type-A personality leaders like Steve Jobs and Richard Branson. It's a skill anyone can learn, one that gets better with practice. One simple way to start is to identify what specific problem people had prior to using your organization's services and then paint a picture of how your service has improved their lives.

Start now.

How You Relate

Likewise, you should strive to understand how your market understands *you*.

When automotive vertical site *Edmunds.com* was trying to better understand the people who use their service, the team reviewed millions of comments online to figure out how people were talking about specific cars. Toyota Corolla kept coming up associated with "college"; the Nissan Sentra was associated with "mom" and "daughter."

Formerly the realm of heavy data processing tools, this kind of evaluation is a lot easier these days with social media monitoring tools like Sysomos. Even starting with a simple tag cloud — where the words that are most commonly associated with your company appear in a larger and heavier font the more frequently people use them — can help you understand how your market views you, the quality of your products and how they are using them.

Language

Starting today, you should strive to eliminate "corporate-speak" from as much of your organization as you can. True, there are some places where this simply won't be possible because of regulatory requirements — financial and material disclosures, for example — but in most places, your words can probably be made more human.

This can even be something as simple as the use of contractions and real human emotions — "Whoa, that's no good. I'll check into that. Thanks for letting me know."

Remember that your stakeholders rely on the people behind the brand to help them when needed.

Empathy

Perhaps the most important factor of building humanity into business is developing empathy. As Jayson Boyers, VP at Champlain College notes, "Though the concept of empathy might contradict the modern concept of a traditional workplace — competitive, cutthroat, and with employees climbing over each other to reach the top — the reality is that for business leaders to experience success, they need to not just see or hear the activity around them, but also relate to the people they serve."

Early in his career, Boyers was responsible for overseeing his company's largest division, which was suffering from poor employee morale and lack of trust in its leadership. "Rather than force my will and clean house," he says, "I sat down with each employee to gauge their feelings about the company and talk about how to improve results. Through empathetic employee engagement, we could create a pathway to success."

Don't fall into the trap of false empathy, though. Many organizations undertake occasional employee or customer surveys to briefly gauge the level of happiness in those groups. Then, they do nothing with the results. Don't use these surveys as a way of trying to fake empathy. True organizational empathy is based on action you take from what you learn. It's worse to ask and then do nothing than to not ask at all.

CHAPTER 3
TOUCH ASSESSMENT

To start, it's helpful to get a sense of your organization's overall humanity — this quick assessment tool will give you your TOUCH score.

TECHNOLOGY

Do you invest in technology that makes things easier for your customers or easier for your staff?
Too many organizations use tools that help achieve internal goals (such as aiming for shorter time on client-support calls) rather than helping your clients and stakeholders with their goals. Think of the difference between Microsoft's software (designed primarily by computer programmers and loaded with features that most people don't use) and Apple's software (designed primarily by human interface specialists, sacrificing some functionality for ease of use).

❑ Our tools primarily benefit us. (0 points)

❑ We don't use much technology.
We are customer-centric. (1 point)

❑ Our tools benefit us and our clients. (2 points)

How many layers of technology do your customers have to go through to reach a human being with front-line decision-making ability?

Web forms, phone trees, and automated marketing certainly make the process of doing business easier, but these technologies often have the "benefit" of keeping your customers and stakeholders further away from real people who can solve problems or handle direct issues. How easy is it for your customers to navigate this technology to get to a real person?

❑ We actively use technologies to reduce opportunities for customers to directly reach a person in our organization. (0 points)

❑ Our processes or technologies permit contact with a staff person though only after first passing through any kind of gate (requiring a call back, entering data into a web form, prescreening on a web chat, etc.). (1 point)

❑ Our customers can reach a real human within one contact point on their first attempt (e.g., during the same call). (2 points)

Do you write a "job description" for the technology you select and conduct annual performance reviews of it?

Smart, human organizations treat their technology reviews the same way they'd review their staff — with annual performance reviews and "bonuses" (more investment in the technology) for tools that perform exceptionally well. This annual review process helps ensure you don't get caught with outdated technology while your competitors race ahead.

❑ We simply don't review our existing technologies on any kind of scheduled basis. We review them only when things go wrong. (0 points)

❑ We do periodically or informally check to make sure the technology is working. (1 point)

❑ We regularly review our business technology to make sure it's still meeting the job description we have for it. (2 points)

OUTCOMES

Adaptability: How do you handle outcomes that weren't part of an original goal?

3M accidentally created their famous Post-it pads when a run of glue didn't hold perfectly well. A staffer started using this "defective" glue on small pieces of paper to attach them to reports. How well does your organization consider these happy accidents as opportunities for new products or customer service channels?

❑ There's no process for discovering and considering new applications that emerge. (0 points)

❑ We have infrequently stumbled upon discoveries that have led to improved processes or new products. (1 point)

❑ We've developed a regular process to escalate potential discoveries for further research. (2 points)

To what degree can *each person* in your organization explain the real-world human benefits you provide to your customers?

Senior executives are usually proficient at the elevator-pitch — a short description of how your organization's outcomes benefit your customers and stakeholders. But how good are your staff at communicating this value outside your firm?

❑ Most of our people just do their job and leave others to explain the benefits. (0 points)

❑ Some keeners are good at communicating how we serve our customer base. Most don't. (1 point)

❑ We train our team members on how to explain to people outside the firm the value we provide. Any of our staff can do this effectively. (2 points)

Does your organization have a simple mantra that clearly articulates your values?

Most organizations have mission statements — unfortunately, they're usually lengthy diatribes that wax eloquent about wanting to be "the leader in innovative products and services" or other such meaningless text. Does your organization have short external-facing text that clearly explains what the outcome of hiring your firm will bring your customers?

❑ We don't have any kind of mission statement, or if we do, our average employee can't tell you what it is. (0 points)

❑ Our mission statement is public, lengthy, and tries to be all things to all people. (1 point)

❑ We have a simple, clear, and short mantra that articulates the value we provide to customers. (2 points)

UNIQUENESS

Can each of your people articulate what legitimately distinguishes you from your competition?

Many businesses believe they distinguish themselves by declaring they "have a superior product." Others have a product so good, they can identify themselves by values and the product sells itself. Some, like Starbucks, have a program that offers a college education to its employees. If your people can't articulate what sets you apart from the competition, you're sunk before you even start.

- ❑ We're not sure if we're different/better than our competition. (0 points)

- ❑ We can add value that our competitors can't, though many people on our team have a hard time articulating this difference. (1 point)

- ❑ Part of our staff onboarding and continued training includes a detailed explanation of why we excel over our competition. (2 points)

To what extent is your employee benefits program customizable for each employee's unique personal needs?

It's a truism that organizations trying to attract top employees can't rely on salary and a basic benefits package. Employees lead complex lives outside of the office, and to get the best people you'll need to offer a more human approach to benefits — one that is customizable to their specific lifestyle and needs.

- ❑ We offer a single, standard benefits package for all employees. (0 points)

- ❑ We can make small adjustments to our benefits offerings depending on each employee's situation. It's not an easy process so it happens infrequently. (1 point)

- ❑ Each employee has their own unique benefits package, negotiated with them on hiring, that suits their own unique life requirements. (2 points)

35

Does your organization have a unique and distinct voice in the market?

You can tell a Nike ad without seeing the logo. You can identify an Apple commercial without watching to the end. Does your brand have its own unique identity that doesn't require a visual or auditory clue?

❏ We don't have, or avoid having, any kind of unique personality in our branding and advertising. (0 points)

❏ We consider our brand to have a personality, with no clear guidelines of how it is to be communicated in our marketing. (1 point)

❏ We have a distinct personality which any prospective client should be able to identify even without seeing our company name or logo. (2 points)

CLARITY

Does your intranet's page about benefits use simple language about how to qualify for and use benefits?

Often, one of the most poorly communicated aspects of business is the most important — communications with your internal staff. One bellwether of clarity is how well you communicate what you offer to your own employees (after all, if you can't speak properly with your own team, you'll have a hard time speaking externally).

❏ We don't have any information about benefits on our internal web server. (0 points)

❏ Our benefits plan is detailed somewhere internally, though it's not easy to find and/or is just a copy-and-paste from our benefits provider's boilerplate. (1 point)

❑ Our benefits packages and how to use them are clearly spelled out internally, exploiting the same personality and voice we use to communicate externally. (2 points)

Are your legal letters friendly in tone?

Writing legal letters (regarding trademark violations, human resources terminations, etc.) is a necessary part of business. But that doesn't mean yours have to sound like a mean-spirited robot wrote them. You'll always get better results when you communicate with human empathy.

❑ We use standard boilerplate legal text, written only to extract results for our organization. (0 points)

❑ We try to use less "legalese" in our letters though we're more comfortable keeping everything in a standard legal form. (1 point)

❑ We always try first to resolve legal issues informally — with a friendly phone call and follow-up email when appropriate. (2 points)

Are your news releases devoid of jargon and over-excited announcements?

Review your last four news releases. If any contain an executive quote about how "excited" you are to be "announcing" something, you're failing to communicate in a human manner. Too many news releases read more like long ads than media missives. How well do you fare?

❑ Our news releases follow a standard form that hasn't changed much in years. (0 points)

❑ We try to avoid jargon and awkwardly inserted expressions of executive excitement but still distribute news releases through traditional channels. (1 point)

❑ We write different versions of our news for different platforms — a short version for employees to post on social channels, longer explainers for the media, and so on. (2 points)

HUMANITY

To what extent do you permit your employees to factor their gut feelings into your RFP evaluations?

Vendor responses to RFPs are usually evaluated based on price, ability to do the work, and reputation in the market. Sadly, many organizations don't have a way to factor a "gut feel" into the evaluator's final decision. Did they get a bad vibe from the vendor's account manager? Often, that's as important as the numbers.

❑ There's no mechanism for considering intuition in our vendor review process. (0 points)

❑ Our staff consider their intuition informally. (1 point)

❑ Intuition is a part of our review process; our team members are encouraged to factor their gut feel into decision making. (2 points)

Does your marketing team have a clear personality profile of each audience segment?

It's hard to identify with humans as customers if you're viewing them only as companies you serve. Companies don't make purchase decisions — people do. How well does your staff know the type of person likely to be a customer?

- ❏ We think in terms of selling to companies, not to humans. (0 points)

- ❏ Our team has the mindset that people, not companies, buy what we sell. (1 point)

- ❏ We have distinct personality profiles of the customers we are trying to attract and understand those customers beyond their professional life. (2 points)

Is the language you use in your written communications the same as you might hear in a conversation?

Too much business communication uses an outdated formality that removes the humanity from the text. How well do you use human language?

- ❏ We write in a purely formal business fashion (i.e., long sentences, no contractions, etc.). (0 points)

- ❏ We try to write less formally, though we do so in an inconsistent manner. (1 point)

- ❏ Our writing uses human language, short sentences, and contractions across all our materials, both external and internal. (2 points)

TOUCH ASSESSMENT SCORECARD

0 to 8.5

Your business is operating in very dangerous territory. Your organizational humanity is barely registering with your stakeholders and you could be losing many customers and employees without even realizing it. You need to make building TOUCH into your business a top priority.

9 to 15

You're good in some areas and lacking in others. It's very likely your customers are frustrated at certain points dealing with your organization. Initiating a review of all places where you deal with stakeholders, and gauging the level of humanity would be a worthwhile exercise.

15.5 to 22.5

The people who deal with your organization may feel like your organization has a split-personality. In some areas, you're exceptional — dealing with people *as* people and keeping a high TOUCH relationship. In others, your stakeholders are feeling like you're dropping the ball and they're not valued. You need to shore up those areas where you're failing and further invest in those where you're doing well.

23 to 26.5

You're in a strong human position though a few gaps exist in your organization's humanity. It's worth doing a quick check into each aspect of your business and asking your stakeholders how you can do even better. While not an urgent priority, this work will serve your organization very well in the long-term.

27 to 30

You're part of a very human organization — kudos! Look for opportunities to further establish TOUCH inside your organization and in the public eye. You can be a trend-setter.

CHAPTER 4

LEADERSHIP

I like you, Lenahan. I see in you things I see in myself... in particular,
a spiritual quality that recognizes there must be more to human
existence than the single-minded accumulation of obscene amounts
of wealth at all costs. Which is why I've called you here today: to
impress on you the absolute importance of ensuring that spiritual
quality never, in any way, shape or form, finds voice in this company.

HUMANITY IS A LEADERSHIP ASSET

I define a leader as anyone who holds him- or herself responsible or accountable for finding potential in people or processes.[5]
— BRENÉ BROWN, RESEARCHER AND AUTHOR OF *DARING GREATLY*

Few things have put pressure on organizational leaders as profoundly as digital communication, particularly social media. The evolution of digital culture, with real-time scrutiny and in-the-moment humanism, has demanded leaders of all shapes and sizes of organizations embrace a new era of open, honest, and real interactions, whether in person or online.

Yes. Both are possible. Both are happening. Dismiss them at your own peril. There are already community leaders, political leaders, and business leaders who have successfully applied their innate interpersonal skills from in-person interactions to their interactions over email, blog posts, text messages, photographs, Facebook updates, LinkedIn posts, tweets, audio podcasts, videos, and more. It's happening all around us.

The most significant barrier to adapting to this new model of leadership is overcoming established norms for leader conduct.

For many years, before free agency, baseball players and fans shared a fairly close bond. Baseball players were human beings, accessible both in terms of being members of the communities for which they played and of having a lifestyle and career that was within reach of the average fan. The business of baseball, encompassing free agency and television revenues, created and progressively widened the divide between the average fan and their on-field heroes. Suddenly, both the players and the hope of becoming a professional athlete seemed inaccessible.

Community, political, and business leaders seem to have gone through a similar evolution. As organizations and aspirations grew in scale, there seemed an increasing distance between the average person and the top brass. Open-door policies were more about perception than reality. They lacked follow-through and often seemed to haunt the career of the person who was bold enough to test the policy.

Social media has done more than just introduce the notion that there is a shorter distance between the average person and a leader of any sort. It has challenged the very way leaders must conduct themselves.

Sincerity and vulnerability, long found in the liability side of the ledger, have fast become valuable assets.

It's been said leaders are in their role because they hold themselves to a higher standard. As social norms have evolved, the standard is becoming increasingly human (we expand on this topic later in this chapter).

Rewards for Being Yourself

Peter Aceto agrees there is a perception that many leaders lack human qualities. In his role as the President and CEO of Canadian bank Tangerine (which operated as ING Direct Canada until April 2014), he is one of a growing number of leaders whose style allows a human organization to flourish. He's also cracked the code of human interactions online.

"I've come to the determination that I will be a better leader inside our organization, and outside for our customers, if I'm real and authentic," Aceto told us. "I empathize with customers who are upset because they're frustrated because we made a mistake or they can't get the answer they want. And I empathize with employees and what it's like to have a young family or to have your father be sick."

Aceto confided that it wasn't his instinct to be real and authentic when he was charting his own career in law and business. He was all too aware of what was expected with respect to workplace personas. It was a mentor at ING Direct who sat him down one day for a chat. His mentor listed things he knew about Aceto. The list included difficulties Aceto faced with his father and Aceto's love of hockey. He suggested Aceto allow these things to be known to the people around him rather than trying to appear perfect all the time. Being himself, tearing down the facade, would allow others to be interested in him and more interested in being led by him.

Aceto admits this advice had a significant impact on his success as a leader. "I've been rewarded for being myself in life and in work." He notes that being vulnerable and letting down his facade has created openings for people to trust him.

If people don't trust you, your marketing won't be worth anything. This is another lesson Aceto learned, one that tested his leadership and relied heavily on his style.

ING Direct Canada ran an ad campaign for their Registered Retirement Savings Plan (RRSP) product in January 2013. Research suggested RRSP season caused Canadians to feel anxious and stressed about the decisions ahead of them, so the campaign hinged on ads portraying people who looked overwhelmed with an ailment identified as "RRSP" which ING would help cure. The TV spots were posted online.

The ads were not well received. Not long after they were released, people, particularly those who are affected by mental health issues, expressed their disgust at the ads, saying they were in poor taste. While depression was not directly stated in the ads, it was clear the ads suggested that idea. In addition to the online backlash, Aceto personally received emails from people whose loved ones had suffered from mental illness and had taken their own lives. Gut-wrenching emails.

Aceto made the decision to pull the ads and issue an apology six days after the ING campaign was launched. He's pleased with and proud of having made that call and notes five specific facts regarding his decision to pull the ad.

1. It was the right decision. Aceto and ING never meant to offend anyone and they didn't foresee the offence. Had they, the campaign would not have run.

2. It was a costly decision. Aside from a misspent marketing budget, there was a negative impact on ING's sales of RRSP products that season/year from both the criticism and the missed opportunity to market their products.

3. The decision to pull the ad and apologize was well received and apparently earned Aceto and ING some positive recognition.

4. In hindsight, he should have made the decision more quickly.

5. He and his company are not perfect. They occasionally let people down. When they do, they are obliged to apologize. And they turn it into a learning experience to improve the way they do business.

LEADERSHIP ENCOUNTERS OF ANOTHER KIND

The world came to know Commander Chris Hadfield from December 2012 through May 2013 … and beyond. Hadfield lived aboard the International Space Station (ISS) during those six months, serving as commander for the last three. His breathtaking photographs of our planet and outer space, insightful tweets about life on Earth, and videos of living in space made him something of a celebrity. It was his version of David Bowie's song "Space Oddity" that turned Commander Hadfield into an international space sensation.

What many people don't know is that none of the tweets or videos would have happened if not for Hadfield's son, Evan.

The younger Hadfield worked tirelessly to coordinate social media content from the ISS and interactions between his father and the public. Evan's efforts did something for space travel that hasn't existed in nearly fifty years, since the lunar landings: He helped create a strong bond between the public and the space program.

There's a wonderful metaphor in how he describes public fascination with what he had his father sharing from the ISS.

"Space has historically been beyond the reach of the average citizen," Evan told us. "Now there's the expectation that space is coming within the reach of the average citizen."

We agree. Social media isn't just shortening the distance between ourselves and the potential of a vacation in space because Chris Hadfield showed us how to brush our teeth in zero gravity. It's allowing anyone considering a career at a financial institution or looking to hone her leadership skills to come within reach of people like Peter Aceto.

In fact, it was through social media that we made contact with Evan shortly after his father started tweeting from the ISS.

We admit that it may seem unfair to compare a business operation on planet Earth to an orbiting mecca of technological innovation. What we're really talking about is building a human connection with your audience using whichever on-ramp you can identify. Often, that's about allowing others to see where they fit within the experience. The space example means that when Evan and Chris fielded requests for photos, they were often from people who wanted to see their own hometowns.

"That sounds like an ego thing," Evan dismissed. "Really, what people are saying is 'show me where I am in all of this. How do I look in comparison to this whole world? Where am I in this world of experience? How do I fit in?' That's what we tried to show. We tried to be as inclusive as possible. We tried to look through as many eyes as we could to help people see themselves."

Often leaders overlook that all-important part of human communication: the unique quality they, and the world in which they operate, offer to their interested audience.

Notice we said interested audience. Intended audience and interested audience are not always the same. It's important to watch for both in your interactions, be they in person or online.

You might find that your leadership style and skills, particularly once humanity kicks in, will have a broader reach and may even earn the respect of some of your harshest critics. While that may not be your intent, even critics have been known to go to bat for their adversaries if they believe it's merited.

BECOMING A CHIEF HUMANIZING OFFICER

There are many great examples from the formative days of social media that illustrate the importance of the human touch in organizational culture. Perhaps because they were so groundbreaking, they often find themselves repeated in books within this genre.

Take the example of tech enthusiast Robert Scoble. He was a frequent contributor to some online support groups for Microsoft software dating way back to the early 2000s. During that time, he also blogged about Microsoft and its products — sometimes his posts were positive, sometimes critical. His contributions proved so valuable, Microsoft hired him to, essentially, continue blogging and producing short video pieces as he had been doing.

Outside of honouring regulatory restrictions on the reporting of financial and leadership information, Scoble's posts didn't require the approval of a legal committee or review board. They went live on Microsoft's website without any corporate review. Even when they were critical of Microsoft.

In that way, he had earned the unofficial title of Chief Humanizing Officer.

Scoble put a human face on Microsoft because he was empowered by the company's leadership to speak as a real person.

SPEAK WITH A HUMAN VOICE AND YOU'LL HAVE TAKEN MORE THAN ONE SMALL STEP.

Pope Francis seems to have embraced the role of Chief Humanizing Officer within the Catholic Church. While we can't speak to how he runs things inside the Vatican, or how some people might view the pontiff's approach to the church, we're particularly taken by how the pope seems to have embraced many of the concepts we're presenting in this book.

The pontiff made international headlines when he broke Palm Sunday tradition in 2014. He abandoned his prepared homily to speak from the heart (though the media preferred to use the term "off the cuff") for fifteen minutes. Then, as the Popemobile navigated St. Peter's Square, Pope Francis jumped off (sometimes while the vehicle was still moving) to mingle with the people. The pope posed in selfies with followers. He even accepted tea from someone in the crowd.

Associated Press reporter Frances D'Emillio wrote, "The pope wants to put people on the margins of life at the centre of the church's attention."[6] He's doing exactly that. And he's doing it by being a Chief Humanizing Officer.

Modern leaders are often celebrated not because of the status bestowed upon or assigned to them, but because they make it possible for us to see ourselves in them.

THREE PHRASES TO REFINE

Leaders are responsible for setting the overall direction for an organization. While tools like business plans and KPIs certainly help, the most powerful tool a leader has at his or her disposal is their own personality. It's how they present their values, model behaviour, and build (or destroy) relationships.

Leaders present their personality largely through their voice, tone, and messages. Which makes it incredibly baffling that, despite a growing number of high profile case studies, many leaders lack the ability to speak with basic candour and clarity.

We see this gap in voice primarily with two of the most important phrases in human communication — acknowledgements and apologies.

Thank You

Mark took bar mitzvah classes. (That's right. Jewish boys don't just magically become men when they're thirteen. They take classes first.)

He remembers one very important lesson he learned from the cantor[7] of his synagogue, David Aptowitzer. He was tasked with preparing Mark to lead the Saturday morning service which would propel him into adulthood.

Part of the process was writing a speech that explained the Torah reading for the service and related it to Mark's thoughts on becoming a young Jewish man. Most importantly, it was imperative he thanked his family, friends, and community for helping him reach this day.

Mark was proud of the draft of his speech, certain Cantor Aptowitzer would fawn over his brilliance and have his four classmates assemble to hear him recite his masterpiece.

That's not what happened.

You've probably never seen so many red marks on a piece of paper before. Cantor Aptowitzer grumbled about inaccuracies in the telling of the story and expressed his disappointment that the analysis was weak at best. Then he stopped at one particular spot as though he had hit a brick wall. He looked Mark straight in the eyes and pointed at some text.

"I'd *like* to thank ..."

He asked if Mark would, in fact, be thanking the list of people that followed or if he was only considering it. It was a Yoda moment: "Do or do not. There is no try." The teacher was unambiguous. There would be no "wanting" to thank people under his watch.

So it came to be that Mark dropped "wanting."

And, as it is written: *there was evening and there was morning.* One lesson.

At issue is how we take liberties with the English language. "I want to thank ..." has become "leaderspeak" for actually thanking an individual or a group of people. It's become part of the vernacular because we've heard it so often. Hearing is believing, perhaps. We don't recognize the not-so-subtle twist that calls into question the sincerity of the thank-you.

Once you embrace this idea, you'll be amazed how often you hear executives, politicians, and other public figures use this noncommittal language in their thank-you messages. On some occasions it is clearly an innocent mistake. On others, you'd swear the communication folk chose their words very carefully to deliver some messages and avoid delivering others (which is a delivery of its own).

"Wanting" to thank somebody is sadly wanting in sincerity. And, it gets worse.

"But": The Anti-Thank

Mark hadn't considered the impact of the word "but" until he and his wife, Andrea Ross, went for premarital counselling. Their family therapist explained that "but" is an exclusionary word whereas "and" is inclusionary. He converted Mark into the cult of "every 'but' can be replaced with an 'and.'"

Consider the phrase "Thanks, but you didn't have to do that." It's a perfect illustration of how the "but" disqualifies the initial "thanks" and chases it with a "no thanks." The second part of the phrase seems to suggest the speaker doesn't really appreciate whatever was done.

Now consider the phrase "Thanks, and that was completely unnecessary." Suddenly the appreciation of what was done and the fact that it was unnecessary can happily coexist. In fact, you could even remove the "and" and make the statement even more direct: "Thanks. That was completely unnecessary."

The important point here is that both wanting to thank someone and thanking someone with a "but" are noncommittal. It doesn't take much effort to be direct and remove all doubt.

Surprise someone. Next time you or your organization need to thank someone, thank them, full stop. Don't keep talking. Don't drain the humanity from your statement.

I'm Sorry

Leaders don't like having to apologize. They feel it makes them appear at fault, a fallible human being. Apologizing is often done as an act of defiance — or at least as an act of reluctance. They fail to see the value of a meaningful apology as the first act of reconciliation. More importantly, they fail to see the potential to convert a challenge into an opportunity to earn respect. By phrasing their statements in a certain way, leaders convince themselves they've answered to the public when all they've really done is ensured they're in a legally defensible position.

Mistakes are big news. Often the apologies are as well.

Apologies are especially interesting since they come in a variety of forms. There are deflecting apologies: "I'm sorry, but if A didn't do B then I wouldn't have done C."; anti-apologies: "I'm sorry if you were offended."; and woe-is-me apologies in which the apologizers twist things to make themselves appear to be the victims: "I just want my life back." Some apologies are hard to place. Count, among those, the epic apology issued by South Carolina governor Mark Sanford for having an affair and lying about it. He covers a lot of ground and weaves together a number of experiences and people as he fumbles through his eighteen-minute press conference. Apologies can be hard. Dragging them out can only serve to make them harder for you to deliver and harder for the intended audience to follow.

Apologies are important enough for someone to have created PublicApologyCentral,[8] a YouTube library of apologies — good, bad, and diabolical. You'll find the bizarre, two-part "Mel Gibson Accounts for his Drunken Anti-Semitic Tirade,"[9] "Serena Williams Apologizes for Threatening Line Judge at the U.S. Open,"[10] (in which Williams manages to "flip channels" and mug in a way as to distract from her mistake), and the David Letterman segment "Michael Richards Apologizes for Racist Rant at Comedy Club."[11] It's noteworthy that Richards speaks directly to the point and never deflects or makes light of his mistake, even if he does stutter while collecting his thoughts.

THE RIGHT WAY

An effective apology requires the right balance of three critical elements:

- the right words, which involves knowing which words to use and which to leave out;

- the right delivery, which involves using a personal tone and embodying sincerity in the delivery; and

- the right timing, which involves knowing when the apology should be issued.

A MODEL APOLOGY (TO A POINT)

One particularly big SNAFU that received significant media attention was borderline high art. It involved now-former Toronto District School Board (TDSB) Director Chris Spence. He had penned "Without School Sports, Everyone Loses,"[12] an op-ed for the *Toronto Star*, which contained five instances of plagiarism.

It goes without saying this is terrible, particularly given the position Dr. Spence (as he was known at the time) held in the education eco-system. We'll leave the criticism to others.

It was a model apology. It should be studied and understood for its speed, decisiveness, clarity, and undeniable commitments by anyone who thinks they may have to apologize at some point (read: everyone).

Unlike public figures who have reason to be embarrassed by their actions (or at least humiliated for being caught), Spence took ownership of his mistake.

In his published apology, since removed from the Toronto District School Board's website, Spence

- explained what he did: "I wrote that op-ed and — in no less than five different instances — I did not give proper credit for the work of others. I did not attribute their work."

- illustrated how he failed to attribute work because he mixed assignments with other activities and didn't properly track his obligations: "I did research and wrote down notes and came back at it the next day and wrote down the notes."

- highlighted the reasons he should hold himself to a higher standard: "There is no excuse for what I did. In the position I am honoured to occupy, in the wonderful job I do every single day, I of all people should have known that."

- owned his mistake: "I am ashamed and embarrassed by what I did. I have invited criticism and condemnation, and I richly deserve both."

- detailed a plan to better himself: "I intend to enroll myself in the Ethics and Law in Journalism course offered by Ryerson University."

In fact, Spence did something particularly important. He noted that, in his role as director of education, the consequences assigned to him should be more substantial than those assigned by the school board's policy for students.

Spence achieved something significant in his statement. By being quick to acknowledge his mistake, direct and clear in his apology, and by declaring that he will better himself, Spence set himself up for a new and even higher degree of credibility should he follow through on his commitment. He also helped to make sure the issue became "yesterday's news today." At the time, Mark suggested a successful reinvention would lead to a lucrative book deal and professional speaking career.

Alas, it was not meant to be. Spence submitted his resignation two days later[13] after media reports revealed that, among other things, his Ph.D. dissertation also included unattributed quotes.

YOU DON'T NEED A CRISIS

The SWARM section of this book provides a thorough framework for dealing with handling issues and crises. These situations typically involve issuing an apology.

However, an apology does not always need to be in response to a crisis. Sometimes you or your organization can unintentionally offend someone with an offhand tweet or blog post. A crisp, clear apology is definitely merited in these situations. They shouldn't be left to snowball into a crisis that demands media attention. In fact, a prompt and definitive apology can often thwart a crisis.

Courier companies have been the subject of high-profile apologies over the last few years. FedEx, UPS, and other courier companies have been at the centre of videos featuring delivery-people who have applied creative interpretation to the phrase "Handle with care."

One such example involves a FedEx employee captured on video throwing stacks of boxes into the back of her truck. The video was taken on July 24, 2013, and clearly shows the uniformed FedEx employee standing at the back of truck 203 997 JRB laughing while playfully showing a co-worker, not in uniform, how to get distance when throwing the boxes.

The video gained a lot of attention. Very quickly.

FedEx issued a response on YouTube the next day. Shannon Brown, FedEx Senior Vice-President of Human Resources, spoke directly to the camera as though speaking to an individual. Great. He even added facial expressions and vocal inflections. Great. And the video came out fairly quickly. Great. Overall, there is a lot that's very good about this apology.

As good as it was, we believe the apology lost some oomph when Brown closed the entire statement with "I want to apologize to all of our customers for the actions of this individual."

This closing did three things to soften the apology.

First, Brown qualified his apology with the word "want." This is particularly noticeable after he spent so much time being very direct with his language up to that point.

Second, he stopped talking to the viewer and started talking to an auditorium. It's easy to feel Brown forgot he was speaking to a person watching a video.

Third, he redirected attention from his apology to the original misbehaviour of a now-former employee. He dialed us back to the problem and sent us on our way with the original issue in mind rather than his apology.

Imagine the same video. However, rather than closing with "I want to apologize to all of our customers for the actions of this individual," consider if Brown ended with "This unfortunate event does not represent the good work of our committed workforce. I am very sorry. And, thank YOU, for taking the time to listen to me."

Which version are you more likely to remember if the apology video came up in conversation at a later time?

Words Need Backing by Actions

We recall the textbook example of an apology from British Petroleum (BP) CEO Tony Hayward. Hayward began his company's apology campaign on June 2, 2010, in the wake of the Deepwater Horizon disaster in the Gulf of Mexico. The reception of his apology was simultaneously both expected and unfortunate for BP and Hayward because without the historical context, the apology is almost perfect in every other way.

Before we examine the strengths of Hayward's apology, let us present three exhibits offered by Hayward himself that make clear why his apology failed to connect with the public.

- Hayward was quoted as saying on May 14, 2010, "The Gulf of Mexico is a very big ocean. The amount of volume of oil and dispersant we are putting into it is tiny in relation to the total water volume."

- When asked if he was sleeping at night despite the unfolding, cascading crisis of the Deepwater Horizon, *Forbes* magazine reported on May 18, 2010, that Hayward responded, "Yeah, of course I am."

- Hayward's May 30, 2010 attempt at an apology was clearly more self-serving than sincere when he said, "We're sorry for the massive disruption it's caused their lives. There's no one who wants this over more than I do. I would like my life back."

It seemed that every time Hayward had opened his mouth to this point, he gave his critics — even his supporters — good reason to shudder. Much of the disbelief played out online, including on the comical parody Twitter account @BPGlobalPR.

@BPGlobalPR — May 23, 2010, 3:52 p.m.
Catastrophe is a strong word, let's all agree to call it a whoopsie daisy.

@BPGlobalPR — May 23, 2010, 4:11 p.m.
Please do NOT take or clean any oil you find on the beach. That is the property of British Petroleum and we WILL sue you.

By the time Hayward issued what appeared to be that earnest June apology, any sincerity on his part was largely rejected by the public. If not for the mishandling of the oil leak by BP and Hayward's perceived absence of communication charisma, the following would have made his apology welcome and appreciated.

The first thirty-three seconds of his video apology deals with the spill and a summary of what BP had done productively to that point. There are many who would argue with the claims Hayward made, except to note that he does open the video with the statement "The Gulf spill is a tragedy that never should have happened." It's attention-getting because it acknowledges what everyone was already thinking and saying, even if some will feel there was a calculated decision by Hayward to leave out mention of BP in that statement.

The strength of the apology kicks in around the thirty-four second mark.

"To those affected and your families, I'm deeply sorry.... To all the volunteers, and for the strong support of the government, thank you."

Notice Hayward delivers a clear and inclusive "I'm deeply sorry." By saying "To those affected and your families," Hayward leaves the apology open for everyone who lives on the Gulf and, arguably, everyone who is affected by the Gulf oil spill.

He also gives an unqualified thank-you to those who volunteered with the cleanup effort and to the U.S. government. He doesn't "want" to thank these people. He thanks them. Full stop.

In the end, actions speak louder than words, and communication failures trump successes. Hayward misplayed his hand and that of BP. The online masses made that known.

ROBOTS AND LEADERSHIP

Guy Hoffman tells a fascinating story about how he came to design and build "robots with soul." His story begins with being inspired by Pixar's animated short film *Luxo Jr.* You may have seen it. *Luxo Jr.* was meant to showcase some amazing advancements in computer-generated imagery. However, like all Pixar projects, the magic is in the human-relatable story. Technology, as amazing as it is, serves as a mere backdrop to this story.

Hoffman wanted to make it possible for people to have the same kind of real life interactions with lamps as were presented in *Luxo Jr.* — the ability to share a knowing look, to play and work together. He did. And he's done much more than that. His robotic creations use technology to mimic moments of emotional connection. He builds personality into his robots, giving them the ability to groove to music in human-familiar ways and participate in free-form music collaboration, including predicting music structure and connecting with other participants in the performance.

What's most remarkable is how people respond during their interactions with Hoffman's robots. His efforts considered two types of robotic brains. He refers to one as the "calculated brain." It functions with a very programmatic and calculated robotic response. The other, he calls the "adventurous brain." It functions more like an improvisational actor who is willing to take risks and interact with the surroundings — willing to make mistakes and correct them.

In his TEDxJaffa talk, Hoffman explains that he invited people to participate in an experiment with the robots.

"I had them do this very tedious task. It took almost twenty minutes and they had to work together, somehow simulating, like, a factory job of repetitively doing the same thing."

It turns out people preferred working with the adventurous robot. They felt it "was more intelligent, more committed, a better member of the team, contributed to the success of the team. They even called it 'he' and 'she,' whereas people with the calculated brain [robot] called it 'it.'"

In another video clip, Hoffman shows an interaction between the adventurous-brained robot and a rapper. In the clip, the robot is bopping alongside the rapper while the rapper is focused on his iPhone, reading lyrics. A few moments later, the robot turns to look at the rapper. The rapper instinctively turns to look at the robot and adds a skip beat to his rap. It's all part of normal performance conduct, yet with a robot that is apparently invested in the experience.

We're sharing this story not to advocate that leaders (or anyone, really) be replaced by personality-infused robots. The key takeaway here is that people preferred working with a robot that seemed more human, that exhibited a personality. People actually felt as though they had formed a partnership with the adventurous-brained robot. Meanwhile, the calculated-brain robot was described as "a lazy apprentice" that did only what it was supposed to do "and nothing more."

The question is, which type of robot leader are you? Calculated brain? Or adventure brain? Guess which one is TOUCH.

ON THE HORIZON

Social Business Is No Longer Optional

As social media and digital marketing become more deeply ingrained in the human vernacular, they will no longer be seen as external to traditional marketing techniques and practices but rather key components in the overall functioning of a business.

Embracing social technology and understanding its functionality and specific role in relation to one's industry will become increasingly important, even for those at the very top, who up until recently have been able to plead blissful ignorance when it comes to how technology and social media is shaping their business's future. Leaders must also be equipped to handle and process an unparalleled amount of big data and know-how to pull meaning and implement actionable items in a fast-moving, highly reactive, and interconnected global economy with new power players and developing nations who are quickly adapting a more Western lifestyle.

Future leaders must have a skill set that encompasses deep digital understanding in order to navigate the complex world of tomorrow, mitigate potential threats, and steer their company or brand toward sustainable profitability. The days of CEOs and high level executives not understanding how technology works or impacts their business are numbered. After all, by 2025, millennials will comprise 75 percent of the workforce. "If 89 percent of them are currently using social media, how can anyone not think that social business will be imperative?" says Jeff Gibbard, president of True Voice Media.

Convergence and Digitization

Leadership always begins with a picture of the future.
— MARK MILLER

The future of business is undeniably digital and convergent, but behind every step we take forward, technologically speaking, there is always a human dimension informing it. Rather than having separate tools to perform specific tasks, we are moving into a realm where our tools are increasingly multifunctional and ubiquitous. Ways of working together that were once thought of as radical (remote offices/ workforces) are now becoming the norm (for better or worse, as we'll learn later in the book). Leaders need to understand the implications of these trends and be prepared to lead a dramatically different team or operation to success along paths that may look nothing like they did ten years ago.

CUSTOMERS, PRODUCTS, OPERATIONS, AND PROCESSES, AS WELL AS ONE'S COMPETITORS, ARE ALL DIGITAL; HAVING THE FORESIGHT OF HOW THAT TRANSLATES AT EVERY TOUCHPOINT FOR YOUR BRAND IS CRITICAL.

NBIC, which stands for nanotechnology, biotechnology, information technology, and cognitive science, continues to transform how we interact and do business. Some experts believe that by 2030, nearly all work will be done in the Internet cloud, where data and applications are hosted on servers which can be accessed from any device, anywhere with an Internet connection. In many ways, we're already there. Convergence — technology that interacts synergistically — will also influence how people run companies from the inside as well as playing a central role in customer-facing technologies (mobile apps, customer relationship management and software systems, and eCommerce). In this race of who can innovate and integrate the fastest, there are destined to be winners and losers in terms of what gets adopted by whom and how quickly, and what ends up becoming obsolete.

In a 2014 *Forbes* story, only 21 percent of business leaders said they have a clear digital vision. Leaders will need to live with a certain amount of uncertainty, as the outcomes of NBIC innovation are highly unpredictable, and must remain sensitive to society's general reaction to radical technological leaps and adoption patterns.

Emphasis on Human Dimension of Employees and Collaboration

The adoption of technology and the population that is online continues to shape how we work and how leaders lead. The pervasive nature of cloud computing, collaborative/mobile work applications, and a stronger emphasis on work-life balance render the concept of "private" or "personal" time much more hazy.

As we continue amalgamating our public and private lives, the onus will slowly shift onto employers to provide a work environment that celebrates and respects the personal lives of their employees and to modify policies to allow for a more transparent border between work-life separation — or connection, depending on how you look at it. Flextime and work-from-home days are already part of many employee packages in a number of progressive corporate environments and are bound to become the rule rather than the exception, with more and more companies adopting virtual arrangements. This needs to be carefully measured for productivity gains, though — as we'll point out later in the book, the trend to move workers out of traditional office spaces sometimes backfires.

TOUCHPOINTS: FIVE LEADERSHIP TAKEAWAYS

 It is possible to use social media and other technological tools and platforms to convey your human side. It's not rocket science. It's about being who you are in person, online. People are already doing it, from students to business leaders.

 The digital age has complicated human decisions with shiny technology, making the path to successful outcomes less clear. If you have identified and embodied human values in your organization, a path will appear. And you'll be better equipped to navigate the rough patches.

 Trailblazers are often showcased and sometimes skewered for challenging the way things are. If it wasn't for them, we wouldn't see ourselves in bank presidents, astronauts, and religious leaders. By being genuinely you, you can help people see more potential in themselves.

 Messages worth delivering are worth delivering well. Don't spin or sanitize your message. Be direct, use words people understand, and take only the time necessary to be understood.

 People relate to other people and the embodiment of human qualities. While we do like our devices and align ourselves with particular brands, there's nothing quite like sharing a moment. Why else would researchers be so interested in creating human-like robots?

CHAPTER 5

COMMUNICATIONS

As a matter of fact, I <u>do</u> have some strong views
about ghost-written blogs.

FIRESTARTER

Mark's "cousin-in-law," Patrick, gathered up some VHS tapes of Christmases and family gatherings dating back to the 1970s. He emailed his mother a short time later to enthusiastically tell her, "Just watched old home movies from when we were kids. Now I'm going to burn them."

Aunt Barb was stunned. "Thanks a lot, Pat," she wrote back sarcastically and more than a bit hurt. "You must have really enjoyed your childhood."

We love how each so easily misunderstood the other; Aunt Barb thinking Pat's digitizing of home movies was a cathartic destruction of family history, and Pat thinking his mom would be pleased that he had such great memories they were worth immortalizing. (It all worked out in the end and copies of the DVD were circulated, complete with footage of Mark's wife toddling around in cozy one-piece pyjamas.)

Misunderstandings are often the rule, not the exception, in digital communication. Language is nuanced by emotions, grammatical devices, and generation gaps. Character counts and other constraints lead to creative use of language to communicate ideas in limited space.

The push for being genuinely "you" on the Web hasn't made understanding any clearer. Sarcasm, wit, and emotions don't transmit. Even emoticons have become ambiguous.

Clarity is playing an increasingly important role in online communications. Strategists and tacticians need to be vigilant about ensuring online messages are easily digestible, unambiguous, and memorable.

This chapter considers some incredibly easy and important changes you can make to humanize your online voice.

THE BIRDS AND THE BEES

Let's start with the birds and the bees. (Don't worry, this will be different than the talk you got when you were ten.)

Traditional corporate communications operates much like a flock of geese — one goose flies in front and the rest obediently follow behind.

Think of the way a news release gets issued in your organization. You put out the news release to the media, who are expected to pass it along to the public, who hopefully pass it along to other interested people.

To be fair, this top-down approach can be effective, and is in some cases — like when issuing financial statements — required by law. This approach is not as effective over more human channels like Facebook and Twitter.

Rather than thinking of yourself as the front bird in the flight, consider how bees do their work. Inside a hive, there is a boss (the queen bee) who moves among the worker bees. She has great respect without needing a magnificent view from the top of the hive.

Likewise, in human social channels, you should position yourself like a queen bee.

Here's how that works in practice. Rather than flying in with missives posted to your social channels, be part of the dialogue. Lurk, listen, add occasional short comments even if someone hasn't asked a specific question. Doing this will help stakeholders come to understand your role as being supportive of them rather than as simply talking "at" them.

Humans want to communicate with other people, not with brands.

Voice

A word about voice: There is simply no excuse for corporate-speak in today's world. You know the style: "DGW Corporation is pleased to announce the release of its innovative, category-leading blah blah blah."

Regardless of the type of business you're in, your brand needs a personality. To be clear: This doesn't mean you need to employ a quick-witted, casual tone with all your communications. Some communications, especially within regulated industries, still require a modicum of conservative language.

But how you speak in the social channels can make a big difference in people's perceptions of your brand.

To see a hilariously executed example, check out the customizable news release from Opera Software at *http://touchthebook.com/opera*. At first loading, the news release looks sadly familiar — riddled with overenthusiastic jargon.

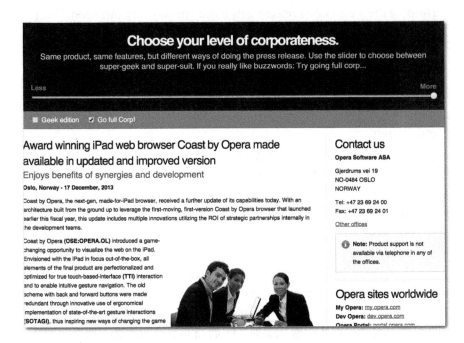

But take that slider at the top of the news release back to "Less" and you get a much more human-readable form of the copy:

Especially if your objectives include getting the attention of journalists, speaking in a clear, human tone will go a long way to keeping your release out of the trash bin of their email account.

THE HUMAN MEDIA

You can't just pump out a news release anymore and expect it'll gain traction. News is increasingly being shared across social networks, and communicating there requires a much more nuanced approach. In short, you need to bring humanity into the development of your media communications.

We've both consulted with national brands in developing a more human approach to this tactic. Here are the seven best pieces of advice to making your communications relevant in a social and human age.

1. **Be genuine.** First and foremost, know that people relate to other people. Since social media allows you to connect directly with the public, be sure your updates (no matter if they're text, audio, photo, or video) speak to people. Don't think or "speak" in headlines, media releases, or talking points. Think and speak coffee shop. This means balancing your corporate messages with being a real person (perhaps with a family) immersed in a complicated, busy world. Also, once people realize your organization is full of other real humans like themselves, they'll think of you more as a human organization rather than a balance sheet and will (generally) be more forgiving when you make a mistake online. Being genuine gets support and attracts the sharing of your online content by others. You want to be genuine. You want to be shared.

2. **Elevate quality over quantity.** Your customers and stakeholders are following the social media activities of several brands, not just yours. Journalists, analysts,

pundits, and enthusiasts will be following more than that. You should strive to ensure your updates are valuable and interesting for the public (even the fun ones). This also means making sure your content is sufficiently unique on each social networking site to make each worth following. If you put out too much content that doesn't resonate with the audience, you will be ignored as noise. You want to be signal.

3. **Engage.** Social media has spawned a culture which expects more from participants than just fresh, self-serving content. Companies need to engage with people during their marketing campaigns. This means following the conversation about your brand, your competitors, and your colleagues. Follow journalists who are covering your space and the people in your market. Look for opportunities to converse with them the way you would during a door-to-door visit. These conversations may be about the election or the local peewee hockey league your daughter is in. Remember, think coffee shop.

4. **Make your content share-worthy and shareable.** Tweets can be retweeted. Photos posted to Flickr can be linked to or downloaded and used on other websites. Videos uploaded to YouTube can be linked to or embedded on other people's websites and social networking accounts. That's not enough. If your content doesn't resonate with people who see it, they won't share it. It must be "share-worthy." Photos that inspire people, videos that educate and entertain people, text that's snappy and engages readers, all of these and many more types of content grease the wheels of the social-sharing machine. They help increase awareness and attract more community members.

One more thing to consider: You should make it easy for others to promote your content by featuring

Share This icons (and the supporting functionality) on your website. You get bonus points for any content you make available under a Creative Commons (CC) licence.

We included a brief mention of CC in the clarity section of chapter two. Let us expand that introduction.

By law, the creator of any original work is, by default, granted an exclusive "all rights reserved" licence to enforce as they choose. Works that are all rights reserved cannot be shared or republished without express written permission from the copyright holder.

CC is a non-profit organization that makes it easy for copyright holders to create licences that provide terms for the sharing and republishing of the work in question. Rather than forfeiting copyright ownership, CC allows the creator to specify which rights he or she retains. A commonly used CC licence allows the end-user to use the content in their own works or to share the content with others, provided this is done so with attribution and not for commercial gain. In this way, the copyright holder eliminates one level of administration, requiring use requests only in the event the end-user intends to use the work in a product or service from which they will make money.

5. **Share other people's content.** If you notice links to other people's content or stumble onto interesting articles, videos, and photos, mention them and provide links from your website, blog, and/or social networking accounts. It's a great way to help your own community and get the attention of the people whose content you're promoting. Plus, it shows that you're on the lookout for great information, that you're part of the ecosystem.

6. **Know how to measure success and whom to tell.** Don't bother telling the media or public how well you're doing online. Don't publicly announce how many followers

your Twitter account has, how many people "like" your Facebook fan page, or how many views your video has accumulated. Population doesn't equate to purchase intent, and saying or suggesting so shows how little you know about social media. Success metrics should be connected with specific campaign goals and be shared with your marketing team. Start by measuring engagement and the outcome of calls to action. If you're successful online, people will be reading, replying to, and rebroadcasting your content, clicking on your links, volunteering, and donating.

7. **Connect the dots.** All of your online activity should be connected, ideally in a hub-and-spoke model. That is, your website should be your content headquarters. Then, your chosen social networking and digital media accounts become outposts which direct viewers back to your website. So, be sure all of your accounts have complete information about your brand to help identify you (this includes a proper description and photo) and a link back to your website. Make it easy for your constituents to find and follow you.

Deploy Your Army

It's surprising how many companies forget that their best brand ambassadors could easily be sitting in their own offices. Happy, engaged employees are often most willing to share your company communications with their social networks (online and off-line) if you ask.

This can be done simply.

Next time you have some news to distribute, send three different versions to everyone in your office: a full-length news release, a 400-word version (for posting on Facebook), and a 125-character version and a link to the news release (for posting on Twitter, leaving enough room for the link). You'd be surprised how many people will share it for you.

But don't stop there. A number of platforms are emerging to help you reward your team members for sharing and capturing analytics about how well the effort is going.

One clever platform is Meevl.com. You start by inviting your employees to participate. They get an email listing your most recent social network posts, and you can also prompt them to post something specific. Directly in the email is a link for them to tweet or post to their own social channels. Meevl then tracks each posting and determines your most frequent posters. The more they share your news, the more points they earn, moving toward rewards for top performers. Because each post is tracked, you could also set up monthly competitions among teams to see which team is best at spreading the word.

There is a danger with these options, though — when letting people post to their own channels without any kind of review process, you're at the mercy of their ability to represent the brand the right way. While some tools (Meevl included) let you review posts prior to their going live, a more human approach is to communicate to your team that you trust their judgment. Train on brand and tone first, then trust that they'll do well. In the event that something goes awry with the positioning of their post, simply (and gently!) remind them of your organization's tone and values. Hire smart people and they'll get this naturally.

THE ONLINE CRISIS PLAYBOOK

People don't ask questions; they just pass judgments.
— MARC MESSIER, OTTAWA FIRE SERVICES

It's bound to happen — things will go bad. Someone on your team will accidentally tweet something personal on your corporate account, or a well-meaning Facebook post will be judged insensitive by the community.

The two keys to recovering from this kind of incident are *humanity* and *speed*. You'll need to respond as soon as you can — even if this means doing so on the weekend or after hours. One way to immunize yourself against these kinds of issues is to establish an online crisis playbook. This can be as simple as a few pages identifying who'll respond and how, or as comprehensive as a one-hundred-page binder which includes holding messages, escalation procedures, and how to activate a crisis team.

Here are some key points on setting up your own online crisis playbook.

Form a Crisis Team

Know ahead of time who'll be responsible for determining how to respond to a crisis. Your crisis team should be composed of the most senior communications person you can spare, representation from legal/compliance, and someone who knows the on-the-ground mechanics of posting to your channels. Your team should be small and their direct phone numbers (including home and cell) should be easily accessible via your intranet.

Prepare a Media Email Address

Your crisis may require having a person at the ready to respond to media inquiries. That doesn't mean this person needs to spend their whole day fielding phone calls. Be sure you have an email address (media@ yourcorp.com works fine) which you can direct journalists to. From this email address, respond to incoming questions and don't forget to follow up with reporters if the issue warrants it.

Keep an Active Password List

When something horrible happens, you'll want access to all of your online properties to post your initial response as soon as possible. Don't fall into the same trap that many other organizations have fallen into — *wanting* to post but not knowing the right technical information (like log-in details) to do so. Each member of your crisis team should be kept up-to-date with any changes to log-in credentials. If you're using two-factor authentication (where log-in attempts require entering a confirmation code sent to someone's cellphone), be sure to know how to find the people who have access to the technology where the log-in credentials will be sent. Be sure to keep two-factor backup codes, if the service permits.

Develop Response Scenarios

You want to have potential responses to negative publicity developed before you need them. This involves identifying the most common issues you may encounter and drafting responses for them. In fact, it's a worthwhile exercise to consider uncommon issues that could possibly happen. A situation could unfold which looks enough like the scenarios you imagine, thus ensuring you're much better prepared when they occur.

If a customer's experience with your product or service leaves a bad taste in their mouth, and their recounting of it goes "viral," you want to be in a position to provide thoughtful responses. This means preparing draft messages (as starters) when you are able to think clearly, rather than when you find yourself feeling defensive and under pressure to respond.

Of course, all response drafts you prepare should be considered templates for you to tweak for each issue. The last thing you want to do is sound like you're issuing a cookie-cutter response.

Be Human

It's tempting to fall back into corporate-speak when responding to a crisis. Avoid meaningless statements like "DGW Corporation is currently reviewing the situation. We have no further comment at this time."

It's perfectly okay to respond naturally, as a real person would. Speak in the first person and tell people exactly how you're handling the situation. One example: "I'm so sorry to hear about that. I've brought this to the attention of our customer support team. They are aware of the urgency here. I'll remain involved until they get in touch with you."

Set expectations and deliver on them.

Maintain a Secondary Channel

In the event that your social channels are hacked and you're not able to post to them right away, make sure you have a secondary channel established to send messaging through. It's best that this channel be visually identifiable as genuinely coming from your organization. This means legitimizing it by providing a link to it from your main website and, if necessary, issuing a statement that you will be using this channel for critical communications until further notice. (An additional fail-safe is to have a backup corporate blog hosted through a separate service provider, like on *WordPress.com* or *Tumblr.com*, in case your primary corporate website is compromised.)

CASE STUDY: THE ALBERTA WILDFIRES

There's no way the government of Alberta could have anticipated that the launch of their Alberta Wildfire Info Facebook page would be so timely. Just days after it went live in May 2011, a devastating wildfire destroyed nearly half of the town of Slave Lake.

It was a true test of Facebook as a hub of emergency communication and general information. The page became an important part of the information flow, integrated into established processes rather than an isolated entity. Three staff worked approximately sixteen hours each day to post information coming directly from the central communications authority stationed in the town.

The Facebook page became more than just a broadcast channel, though. The public affairs officers (PAOs) who managed the page made a point of ensuring all requests for information posted to the page received responses. An important part of that process was acknowledging each request and committing to providing quality information as soon as it was available. Then staff ensured that all questions posted to the page were answered with good information in a timely manner.

Besides being a platform for communication about the spread of the fires, damage to neighbourhoods, and the safety of residents, the page became a forum for people to coordinate the housing of displaced animals and establish sites for the collection of donations.

It quickly became a trusted and credible source for the public and media. Among the page's many unanticipated outcomes were that media followed the updates very closely, which may have reduced the number of queries the public affairs and crisis communications team had to field, and that the community of participants self-policed. The latter was particularly important since language and impatience could have easily become unmanageable.

One public affairs officer we spoke with recounted a few occasions when the community defended the PAOs after online postings by some individuals suggested the speed of information was unsatisfactory, a side effect of high expectations in the digital age.

The page was kept busy later in 2011 when fires broke out in Fort McMurray, and it has retained its important status since.

The net effect of the page has been overwhelmingly positive, something PAOs smile about as they recall the difficulties they had convincing managers the tool was a good idea.

THE FIVE PERSONALITIES

Tod's not a jerk. Really, he's not. Although judging from a tweet he sent back in October 2012, you might think otherwise.

He was giving a speech in Seattle and staying at the local Westin hotel. As he often does, Tod had forgotten his razor back home, so he called the front desk and asked if they could send up a toiletries kit. Almost all hotels have them, and most will give one to you free.

The operator said, "Sure, no problem. Twenty-three ninety-five."

By the time he processed what she had said, Tod had already hung up. Twenty-four dollars for a cheap razor? (Maybe if he had been staying at a lower-end hotel, but this was a relatively top-shelf brand. And he was a gold member in its loyalty program.)

So — and here's where the prickish part starts — instead of calling back and asking someone why it was so much, Tod grabbed his iPad and pounded out a brief rant.

@todmaffin — Oct 12, 2010
So @WestinSeattle is charging me $24 for a disposable razor. Every other hotel — even the cheap ones — will give that to you for free! #fail

---

There. That was better. He felt vindicated, smug, and secretly hoped his twelve-thousand-plus followers would retweet it. That would teach the hotel a lesson, he thought — all he needed now was a long moustache to twirl with his fingers while saying "Mwa-ha-ha-ha!"

To its credit, the Westin's headquarters monitors brand mentions of its hotels like a hawk and, within minutes, they had called the front desk of the hotel and had the manager call Tod.

"It's not really a big deal," Tod said, feeling a little sheepish now that he was actually forced to speak with a real human being. "I was just surprised, that's all."

"I think there's been a misunderstanding," the manager explained. "Our operator was quoting back your room number — twenty-three ninety-five — to deliver it to you. That wasn't the price. Of course we wouldn't charge you for a razor."

"Oh," Tod mumbled. "Sorry about that."

An embarrassing misunderstanding.

Like we said, Tod's not really a jerk. But sometimes he plays one on Twitter.

Tod isn't the only one who's popped onto Twitter, Facebook, or a blog to shout angrily at a seemingly unmanned corporate account. Sometimes rants get results, sometimes they get ignored, and more often than not they just end in embarrassment for the person who complained.

This isn't the way it used to be. Before the Internet, even talking to telemarketers was handled with an ounce of decorum.

Today, entire websites exist to collect consumer reviews — many of them harshly negative — and those reviews have the power to bring down entire companies.

Remember that not everyone who posts something negative about your brand is necessarily out for blood.

As a result of client projects for which we've read thousands of comments left on news articles and blog posts, we've organized com-menters into five main categories. The premise is that you must first seek to understand (and believe us, reading hundreds of comments is an important and valuable commitment) before you can decide on any follow-up course of action. You need to become more familiar with what the issue really is and who you should be reaching out to before you put energy into what should be said.

The following are the five categories of commenters we've identified:

- **Involved:** These are the people who are close to or very concerned about the issue at hand. They know the stakeholders, they have intimate knowledge of the contributing elements, and they can analyze the different directions and effects of the issue on the fly. Involved commenters help keep the conversation relevant no matter their stance on the issue.

- **Informed:** These are the people who have taken the time to learn more about the issue and its key players. They tend to know the history and appreciate its impact. Informed commenters generally have a personal interest in the issue. They contribute new ideas to the conversation and help others understand by taking the time to offer valuable responses.

- **Misinformed:** These are the people who have skimmed the article and possibly other resources, may have misunderstood the information they received, and have collected or were fed inaccurate information from other sources. This is the first level of commenter that lets opinion cloud the issue by relying on their own opinions to fill in holes in their understanding. Misinformed commenters aren't necessarily malicious.

- **Uninformed:** This is where the participants in the conversation transition from being people who generally have something to contribute to being commenters who have a need to be heard. The uninformed choose to let their opinion validate their broken logic. They aren't interested in the backstory and don't know who the stakeholders are. In most cases, they've picked up on a single point of the article or taken a single piece of information out of context. Uninformed commenters like to pontificate and are happiest when they deconstruct what other people are saying, sometimes peppering their comments with personal attacks.

- **Angry:** Known in the online community as "trolls" and "flamers," this is the angry mob of people who like to berate others no matter what the discussion is about. It's more often than not the case that they know little about the issue and probably won't come back to it. They spray their anger and leave. This group gets its energy from lobbing emotional attacks that lack, among other things, logic.

The table that follows quantifies five qualities of each commenter category based on several criteria with ratings of one (lowest) to five (highest), with zero indicating "none." The qualities cover engagement (how likely the commenter is to provide more than one contribution); understanding (how much knowledge the commenter has on the issue and its contributing factors); credibility (how much believability and insight the commenter offers in the discussion); logic (how likely the commenter's contribution is to make sense and relate to the issue and its contributing factors); and emotion (how much mood and personal feedback is likely to be present in the commenter's contributions).

THE FIVE COMMENTERS

	ENGAGEMENT	UNDERSTANDING	CREDIBILITY	LOGIC	EMOTION
INVOLVED	2	5	5	4	2
INFORMED	3	4	4	4	3
MISINFORMED	4	3	3	3	3
UNINFORMED	5	2	1	1	4
ANGRY	3	1	0	0	5

Note that the Involved tend to offer their insight and knowledge in a few credible and logical arguments before they depart from the

78

exchange. These people tend to feel their points have been made and don't require repetition. It's hard to keep these people around for a meaningful discussion, particularly when the angry mob gets involved.

Misinformed people tend to stick around more. Our observations suggest many of these people seem genuinely interested in a productive discussion of the issues in order to expand their understanding. They have some credibility in the exchanges because they appear to listen.

The conversation gets much more prickly and unproductive as the uninformed and angry participants become more involved. They're just itching for a fight and will use ad hominem attacks to get a charge out of their targets. They turn the discussion from the issues to the personalities of the participants. And they tend to be reasonably active. They often depart out of fatigue or in protest.

Knowing the qualities of these groups is important. It will help you better prepare your responses, if any are merited, to the conversation.

Remember, you must have a handle on the people in your camp as much as you need to vigilantly watch and react to your critics. Sometimes your greatest informed and misinformed supporters in any category can get testy. To earn credibility, you must protect informed critics from unreasonable supporters as closely as you protect your own interests.

Once you know your commenters by their categories, it becomes easier to figure out who to engage with, how, and when.

MAD-LIB PITCHES AND SOCIAL MEDIA

We've each received many unsolicited pitches from both reputable and unknown sources. There's a long list of stories we could tell. This one is particularly interesting. It involves Mark's wife, Andrea, who is a breast cancer survivor.

Andrea was once pitched by a public relations advisor (Ms. P) about a line of post-mastectomy bras. Ms. P said if Andrea would consider blogging about the bras, she would gladly send along a sample.

While Ms. P may have mined Andrea's email address from her blog, WeCanRebuildHer.com, she had clearly not done her research.

At the time of the pitch, Andrea's most current post was a reflection on having survived breast cancer treatment with both of her breasts. Further, a search of "mastectomy" on Andrea's blog reveals earlier posts when Andrea decided to have a lumpectomy rather than a mastectomy.

Andrea replied to acknowledge the pitch and draw Ms. P's attention to her most recent post.

In a follow-up, Ms. P agreed to send some regular bras (which she generously did). However, she also asked if Andrea might consider blogging about the post-mastectomy line. As Andrea notes, the suggestion was that she review a product not intended for her. Andrea rightfully declined, noting in her email that

> Having not gone through the devastating loss of one breast, or two, and all the associated trauma and psychological adjustment, I would never be so insensitive as to express an opinion on post-mastectomy products.

PR professionals must take care in their pitches. Especially nowadays. It's extremely important (and very easy) to research the people you will be pitching to make sure they are the right people to approach or, if not, whether they might be able to help find the right people. And it's equally important to never ask someone to comment outside their own area of expertise and/or experience.

Andrea and Mark have been actively involved in social media for many years. Their success building communities around content creation, children's books, and Andrea's journey through breast cancer means they are regularly pitched by organizations looking to benefit from their activities. Nearly all of the pitches they receive are like Mad Libs (a writing game in which the player is asked to provide nouns, pronouns, verbs, and adjectives that are placed in a story, often with extremely humorous results).

Even when a pitch is altruistic, it should still be personalized. Social media creators don't appreciate being patronized by statements like "I really enjoy your blog" especially when the very next phrase is something along the lines of "I thought you might be interested in helping us promote our own initiative" or "Your blog is a perfect fit for our client/campaign/product/service."

Andrea has received a lot of these requests because breast cancer organizations and for-profit businesses want a piece of the action, particularly during October, Breast Cancer Awareness Month. The same is true of people who work in the "pink for profit" mindset, all year round.

So, it's time to call out a pitch, share our thoughts on where this pitch went wrong, and offer our top five things to do when reaching out to bloggers.

> Hi Andrea,
>
> I hope you're doing well today. I'm writing to introduce my company, [redacted], which is a leading online service for sharing stories through photos. Your inspiring story and battle against cancer caught our eye. Thank you for the encouragement and comfort you bestow to other women (and men)!

The writer starts off by trying to establish herself as important ("my company is a leading …") before thanking Andrea for sharing her story online. She doesn't get into specifics, which proves this is a form letter. If the author really had read Andrea's blog, she might have congratulated Andrea on soldiering through the most difficult time in her life, congratulated her on her recent return to work, or remarked on that day's self-deprecating post about Andrea getting used to the return of her eyebrows. The only thing the writer revealed is that she knows how to use Google. The writer goes on to say,

> As October is Breast Cancer Awareness Month, we are seeking new ways to help those who have been affected by breast cancer. Today we released a new Breast Cancer Awareness theme for sale in our [redacted]. Through this design, created by breast cancer survivor [redacted], we hope to better enable our community to share stories and support others as you have done via your blog.

Andrea's just been told the writer's for-profit business is selling something and Andrea can now determine that the author wants her help promoting this product to the engaged community Andrea's attracted and earned the trust of. The writer has not yet explained what value the product has for Andrea or her community, only that she's selling something.

> To show our support for this tremendous cause, [redacted] is donating $1 to [redacted] for every purchase of the Breast Cancer Awareness theme throughout October.

Ah … here's the value proposition: The writer will share a very small portion of her revenue with a breast cancer charity. The writer apparently hasn't read Andrea's blog where she self-identifies as a member of the "No Pink For Profit" team in the Run for the Cure.

> Please consider using this digital design to share your own story or to inform your audience about how to help find a cure via [redacted]. We will be featuring all these creations in a community gallery on our site to showcase care stories and to build awareness. For reference, here is our blog post with additional information: [redacted].
> Thank you for your time and please don't hesitate to write back with questions or feedback.

> All my best,
> [redacted]

Community builders work hard to provide value, earn trust, and establish meaningful relationships. They earn social capital and work very hard not to squander it. Those who do it best are selective about what they ask their community for, especially when it comes to hard-earned money. The result is that more people are willing to participate when the call finally comes. For example, Andrea raised $5,700 in sponsorships for the Run for the Cure — all through her website. The writer of the pitch would have to make 5,700 sales through Andrea's blog for Andrea to have the same impact she's already had with her own community.

Which brings us to our final point. Mark followed the link to investigate the process of purchasing the writer's product. It took him to a blog post in which he had to click another link to purchase the product. That link launched a pop-up that took over his whole screen and displayed a catalogue of products from which he had to find the desired product. Once Mark clicked on that link, he had to click yet another link to "purchase credits" to get the theme. That was the point at which he'd seen enough. Aside from everything else, there's only so many hoops an online buyer will go through to complete a transaction.

Top Five Things to Do When Reaching Out to Key Participants in Social Media Communities

1. **Get to know the person.** Don't just Google a blogger, follow their blog for several posts, read posts that have been recently commented on, and randomly select posts to read from the archive. Be sure this is the person you want to approach and know why.

2. **Customize your message.** You need to demonstrate to the recipient that he/she is the right person for you to approach. This is particularly important when you're pitching someone who already gets lots of pitches; you should assume that to be the case for everyone you approach.

3. **Demonstrate value.** This is not about ego or money. This is about being clear to the person that your product has value to him/her and the community they've built. You need to think about whether or not your product solves a problem or allows your pitchee and their community to do something they might not have done or not have been able to do themselves.

4. **Keep it simple.** Make your pitch short and simple. Make the call to action short and simple.

5. **Check for conflicts.** Check to make sure your product doesn't compete with another product, initiative, or personal/community value as indicated on the site. Knowing that allows you to save the opportunity to pitch the blogger at a time when you can count on his/her support.

Yet another pitch directed at Andrea resulted in the unravelling of *PincBox.org*, a commercial venture, despite its *.org* facade. The company and its owner were the target of criticism in blogs, on Twitter, and on Facebook for marketing a high-priced ensemble of stationery and soap as a way, the company suggested, to show its support for those who were going (or had gone) through breast cancer. That is, they sell a product or service packaged in pink (the colour adopted by breast-cancer-related charities) and reportedly committing to donate a small portion of revenue from the sale of their for-profit product to a breast-cancer-related charity. Pinkwashing.

After twenty-four hours of blowback, the owner put PincBox into remission and yanked seven comments critical of her insensitivity and business model. The site subsequently disappeared from the Web.

Clearly, the owner wasn't as familiar with the life-changing experience breast cancer is for patients, their loved ones, and their friends as the people she pitched were. It appeared, instead, that PincBox had been created to make some fast cash from people going through a frightening life crisis. A few minutes of online research would have helped the owner understand that most breast cancer patients and their network of supporters vilify those who use pink for profit. PincBox asked breast cancer survivors, and some who won't know a life without cancer, to help them push a sixty-dollar gift box. Of that, five dollars was reportedly earmarked for an unspecified breast cancer research beneficiary. A blogger name Ann pointed out on her blog that PincBox was probably pocketing a cozy forty-seven dollars in profit on each box.

Among the comments left on the owners' blog on July 12, 2011, were:

- "I speak for many in the blogging community when I saw trying to profit off the backs of suffering women.

I am stage IV, which means I will die of cancer. I don't need a $60.00 box of soap and a journal because you promise to give to cancer research. You intend to make money off the suffering of cancer patients and that is evil. I got a huge community of bloggers and twitter users blogging your scam. Maybe next time, you might want to actually read a blog you come across. But I'm doing my best to put you out of business." — Ann

- "Your pinc box campaign is an insult to anyone dealing with breast cancer. It stinks of GREED and selfishness. Seriously, selling crap in pretense [*sic*] of helping a cause is beyond clueless and smacks of shear meanness." — Patti

- "Does this pinc box include creams that are kind to radiation-ravaged bodies, or lips that are peeling and dry, or products for nails that are chipped and cracked from chemotherapy treatment? What about natural organic shampoos and conditioners for those of us who are trying to grow their hair back without a product full of chemicals?" — Mon

Those who felt passionately about the issue were relieved the message reached the source, who was apparently moved enough to pull down the criticism. More significantly, though, the owner never acknowledged or responded to growing online criticism.

As Mark noted on his own blog, breast cancer and the treatment process are not consumer products; the experience is not for sale. Nor, do we expect, would anybody be keen to pay for it.

DIGITAL EYE CONTACT: THE AHA MOMENT

Democratized media is doing more than just giving everyone the same potential to reach an international audience — it's motivating people to think differently about how they engage with others and, ultimately, bring about meaningful change.

Invisible Children is a charitable organization that was propelled to international superstardom when they launched their KONY 2012 campaign. The campaign challenged many popular conventions regarding how communities are mobilized and activated online. It was a campaign which could be the subject of a post-secondary course. We'll take a decidedly more abridged look at it.

It began with an attention-getting phrase: "Nothing is more powerful than an idea whose time has come ... whose time is now."

What followed broke conventional thought about online communication and activation. Specifically, Invisible Children essentially dared the viewer to watch a thirty-minute video. Or so it seemed. In many ways, it was a series of well-crafted short videos, strung together with clever cliff-hangers, though some might call them scenes and transitions.

The video introduces the horrific reality of Joseph Kony and his Lord's Resistance Army (LRA). For over twenty-six years, Kony has been abducting African children, turning the girls into sex slaves and the boys into child soldiers. However, the video doesn't lay out the situation bluntly and directly. Very few of us would have the stomach for that, and it would make us feel helpless.

Instead, the film's director and narrator, Jason Russell, tells stories and motivates the viewer into realizing Joseph Kony can be stopped. Russell is remarkably effective.

Ultimately, the success of the video can be organized under three broad headings: Alignment, Hope and Action. AHA!

Alignment

Jason makes digital eye contact with the viewer by connecting on a human level. He speaks in the first person, showcases the absurdity of the situation by positioning it through the eyes of children and, perhaps most importantly, makes emotion one of the main characters in the video.

The children Jason introduces are Jacob Acaye, a Ugandan boy he befriended who had managed to elude capture and whose brother was killed at the hands of the LRA, and his own son, Gavin, to whom he tries to explain the bizarre story behind Joseph Kony and his army.

Gavin represents more than just a cute, innocent face; he represents our own confusion in trying to understand and explain atrocities. Jacob represents more than a black child who breaks down when given the opportunity to share what he'd say to his brother if he were still alive; he highlights North Americans' indifference to issues that don't immediately affect our daily lives. In fact, Jason even says at one point, "If my son were kidnapped and forced to kill, it would be all over the news." That's a reminder of a statement made earlier in the video: "If that happened one night in America, it would be on the cover of *Newsweek*."

It's not all about tugging at emotional heartstrings, though. The video connects with the viewer at the point of familiarity with modern technology — social media, specifically. The story is told using the familiar Facebook Timeline as a visual anchor. The mocked-up timeline is used to launch videos that illustrate the unfolding narrative. Russell also hooks us by playing clips from popular YouTube videos that strike emotional chords; clips such as the one of a young deaf woman who hears with her cochlear implant for the first time, and another of the young boy who was rescued from a well he'd become trapped in seven days earlier.

Another way Jason ensured he would capture the audience's attention was by daring the audience to watch the video. "The next twenty-seven minutes are an experiment. But in order for it to work, you have to pay attention." And the countdown begins.

Hope

There's an increasing amount of fatigue and despair being brought about by negative messaging. Whether it's emaciated dogs rescued from a puppy mill or eyewitness video of bombs exploding in crowded metropolitan centres, too much of what we see and experience has established a strong foundation of feeling that any action we take is too little, too late. Sensationalistic campaigns, even when done with a bit of cheekiness, are contributing to a downward trend of meaningful participation. It's no surprise that the most many people will do to participate in change is no more than clicking a link suggesting they "like" something, even if the word *like* is grossly inappropriate in such circumstances.

Jason had a pool of sensationalistic images he could have exploited throughout the video. He chose not to. Rather, he made sure they were included in a way as to make a quick point (eleven images were flashed in three seconds, long enough to register yet fast enough to not make a lasting and disturbing impression) on which he'd rather not dwell. He focused instead on the potential for meaningful change.

A series of lessons learned and successful actions taken are highlighted in the video. Among them, Invisible Children turned a matter that was "simply not an important enough issue on the radar screen of American foreign policy" into a significant policy decision by President Barack Obama — to send troops to support the effort to dismantle the LRA and bring Joseph Kony to justice. The charity raised money and rebuilt schools, created jobs, and built an early warning radio network. They did it themselves "because we couldn't wait for institutions and governments to step in."

Let's restate that. Invisible Children raised the kind of public awareness that motivates policy-makers, and they put their money where their mouth was by actually helping the communities that were affected by Joseph Kony and the LRA.

The hope card is a powerful one. If people believe they are joining something that's already making meaningful progress and that they too can make a difference, they will feel compelled to act.

Action

There must be a payoff to effect change, measurable change. You need a call to action. More specifically, you need simple, scalable calls to action.

Jason grabs the audience by saying, "It's hard to look back on some parts of human history because when we heard about injustice, we cared but didn't know what to do.... If we're going to change that, we have to start somewhere."

He continues by asserting "we know what to do" and issues a rallying cry to make Joseph Kony famous. A plan is outlined to push messaging to and through twenty culture-makers and twelve policy-makers with the goal of getting Kony's name into as many places and into as many heads as possible. The hope is that the more people know about Kony, the more likely the foreign policy and support provided by the American government will remain in place. More importantly, Invisible Children hopes Joseph Kony would be caught and brought to justice by the end of the calendar year 2012.

For those who wish to do more, Jason encourages them to purchase an action kit or donate funds and receive the action kit for free.

The connecting tissue, though, the call for working together to do something remarkable, to be part of something remarkable, would be "Cover the Night." Viewers are encouraged to be part of an event which would see public spaces plastered with KONY 2012 posters to make Joseph Kony's name famous overnight on April 20, 2012.

Social media lit up as the video became part of the consciousness. Word spread like wildfire over Twitter, Facebook, LinkedIn, blogs, online news sites, and other media. Millions of people watched the video. The whole video. Besides being caught by surprise by the speed at which the video became popular, Invisible Children became overwhelmed by the number of visits to their websites, downloads of various stencils for painting the KONY 2012 logo, orders of their action kit, and requests for interviews by international media.

It was the kind of cause-lifting attention and cash infusion most non-profits and non-governmental organizations (NGOs) dream of. It was also the kind of spontaneous superstar status that causes many people in digital culture to look for opportunities to take the sheen off the newly minted superstars.

Within a few days, criticism of the KONY 2012 campaign and Invisible Children's financial statements started to mount. Among the more prominent criticisms were that Invisible Children had oversimplified the story of Joseph Kony and the LRA, that they hadn't presented a complete picture including recent movements by the rebel group, and that they spent a lot of money on travel and creating the movie that could have been better spent on other things such as helping the affected communities.

Invisible Children did not waver. They faced the criticism head-on, publishing detailed information including an item-by-item response to each criticism and posting summary videos featuring CEO Ben Keesey online.

The international superstardom continued. Jason Russell continued to do a barrage of interviews, many of which now included questions about the criticisms the group faced. The pressure mounted and a new crisis grew for the organization. Jason suffered a very public, and somewhat misreported, breakdown. It was a big blow to the organization and invited additional online criticism and satirical commentary.

To their credit, Invisible Children remained very visible. Ben continued to record video statements addressing the crisis and thanking supporters. He appeared worn out as he spoke from what appears to be his heart rather than a script. Ben appeared sincere.

While we can't comment on the quality of the information about Joseph Kony, the LRA, and the activities of the rebel group provided by Invisible Children, we feel their video serves as a good model for galvanizing public interest and action relating to a complex, widely unknown issue. Consider that you don't get children interested in math by throwing calculus at them. You introduce simple addition and subtraction to build the understanding (and hopefully the interest). Leaving out multiplication and division isn't lying or disguising facts. It's part of the iterative process of achieving understanding.

CAREFUL SELECTION AND SIMPLIFICATION OF INFORMATION HELPS PUT AN ISSUE ON THE PUBLIC RADAR AND, WITH ANY LUCK, THE PUBLIC AGENDA.

In this case, too much information would have muddied the message and likely have overwhelmed viewers. Another way to look at it is that Invisible Children raised awareness of an issue in such a way as to arm members of the public with the information they needed to further investigate and arrive at their own considered opinion.

Subway maps are a great metaphor for how to select important information and present it as part of a campaign. They don't show you every detail. They generally include only stops, major intersections, and landmarks, and are rarely even to scale. The point of the map is to show you generally where the subway goes and where it stops along the way.

Invisible Children did that very well. They showed the information you needed in order to arrive at the conclusion that Joseph Kony is a bad man who needs to be stopped. They provided a few methods by which you could actually help stop him. Then they sent you on your way.

It's the combination of all of the elements suggested here that make the KONY 2012 playbook an important addition to your TOUCH library.

Before Invisible Children achieved superstardom, a young woman from Ottawa achieved something similar, on-scale.

Hélène Campbell was eighteen years old when she was diagnosed with Idiopathic Pulmonary Fibrosis — a hardening of the lung tissue. This is a life-threatening condition. Survival, at least life-extension, depends on getting a double-lung transplant.

Rather than sit idly by, passing time in the hopes of one day getting her much needed transplant, Hélène took to social media in the hopes of raising awareness of organ and tissue donation. As she notes, organ donation by a single person can save as many as eight lives.

The turning point came on January 16, 2012 when she posted the video "Help Hélène save lives as well as her own!" to YouTube. In it, Hélène issues an energetic challenge to help get Justin Bieber to tweet about organ donation. It would be a coordinated effort scheduled to take place three days later, on January 19, to promote the video through tweets (and other social media channels) directed to @JustinBieber in the hopes of getting the star's attention. Why?

"Because he has a ton of followers," Hélène notes in her video.

There's an elegant genius to this. Hélène, who goes by @alungstory on Twitter, didn't ask people to sign their donor cards. She didn't ask people to donate money to organ donor charities. Hélène clearly knew that getting people, especially young people, excited about the possibility of getting something noticed by Justin Bieber was motivation enough to draw attention to the issue.

The Trillium Gift of Life Network, a body responsible for administering organ donor registration (among other activities), reported that registrations began to increase as the campaign began. That means Hélène was already raising and converting awareness.

The campaign generated 18,000 tweets on January 19. Not bad considering this campaign came together on three days' notice. By January 20, Trillium reported a 300 percent increase in registrations through their online tool.

The campaign would prove even more successful. Justin Bieber tweeted "@alungstory i got the word … you have amazing strength. i got u. #BeAnOrganDonor" at 3:43 a.m. on January 21. It was the first of two tweets the pop star issued for the campaign that day, helping to drive nearly 40,000 tweets — on a Saturday, to boot.

Trillium refers to the surge in registrations that came in that weekend as "The Hélène Campbell Effect."

Mark has showcased Hélène's video in presentations, asking the audience members what about the video they believe helped drive so much interest, even before Justin Bieber got involved. Without fail, the answer has always been tied to how energetically personable and relatable Hélène appears. One gentleman commented that it was the cutaway to Hélène fussing with her hair that made him realize she could be someone he might know. He further noted the sense that he wasn't being asked to do a random act by a random person. Rather, a sincere human was giving him the opportunity to be part of something bigger than himself. Oh, and he would be checking to make sure his organ donor card was signed as soon as the session was over.

True, Justin Bieber helped bring awareness of the issue to a larger audience. However, the impact of the whole campaign isn't lost on Hélène.

"We don't even need to reach out to a celebrity. Sure it helps with worldwide attention. The fact that just people being aware, jumping on board, have registered online — that's fascinating."

Here's a checklist for pulling together a campaign inspired by Invisible Children's KONY 2012 and Hélène Campbell's organ-donation fundraising project "A Lung Story" playbooks:

✓ **Get personal.** Present your information in human-relatable style using story. Tell it in the first person, using your own experiences as they've been internalized (rather than itemized). That's not being vulnerable. It's being powerful. Real people can identify with that.

✓ **Think subway map.** The information you present should be relevant without extraneous detail. There's a time and place for the minutia. While you're trying to gain public attention and support is not the time.

✓ **Focus on hope and the positive.** Show that progress has been made. If possible, show how previous challenges became opportunities. You want to show potential supporters they're joining a winning team rather than taking a gamble. You do that by leaving the grotesque and sensationalistic imagery out of the campaign.

✓ **Include everyone, or as many people as possible.** Your campaign isn't just about the people leading the organization, the cool people they hang out with, and the celebrities they want to enlist (it isn't your high school yearbook). Your campaign and its success is about everyone, everywhere.

✓ **Give people something meaningful to do.** Present it as a challenge if you must. The more you can get each person to do, the better. So don't structure your campaign around getting the most likes, tweets, or signatures. Focus your campaign on achieving meaningful outcomes. Have your calls to action be in service to those meaningful outcomes.

(Joseph Kony was made famous and many millions of people became aware of a problem they'd never known existed. On May 12, 2012, Ugandan forces captured one of Kony's top four commanders

Caesar Achellam. Unfortunately, Joseph Kony is still at large. Invisible Children's work is not done.)

CASE STUDY: HEALTH-CARE GROUP UNDER FIRE

A national health-care association had mishandled stakeholder criticism for months. This included ignoring questions and concerns posted by the people they exist to serve (their "community" of patients and their supporters) on their official Facebook fan page. There was a general perception that the organization had talked down to their community at public meetings and when quoted in traditional media channels.

The community felt betrayed and abandoned. So they did the only thing they could do to get attention. They conducted what equated to a mutiny — they took over the organization's official Facebook fan page. In addition to posting criticism and ad hominem attacks of senior leadership and the fan page administrator, the community did the public information work on the association. That is, they answered legitimate questions posted by newcomers with relevant and meaningful health-care information. Against better advice, the organization decided to go dark.

This decision and other actions taken by the organization created the conditions to marginalize themselves, allowing the community to not only criticize them but to do the work the organization should have been doing.

Mark was working for a multinational public relations firm at the time and was brought in to help repair their client's damaged reputation and build a new relationship with their online community. He offered the following among other key pieces of counsel:

1. Replace the Facebook fan page administrator. A fresh face would give the organization the opportunity to reset with a new personality not known to the community. It would also get the attention of the community, likely giving the new person a chance if they presented themselves well.

2. Have the new admin work on building relationships with the community and its members. This includes

reinforcing the community participation policies regarding profanity, ad hominem attacks, and other negative behaviour. Because of prior lax enforcement of the policies, a two- to three-week amnesty period during which warnings would be issued would help reframe the conversation and allow people to understand what content crosses a line. The core of this was DO NOT delete anything already on the fan page and DO NOT delete anything during the transition period.

3. Be more communicative with the community, and respond to criticism with grace and dignity. This includes allowing criticism, provided it was presented productively and within the participation guidelines.

4. Harness the passion of the community. Some of the most vocal critics were also the most active when it came to providing relevant and effective health-care information. Harnessing that passion rather than fighting it would ultimately be helpful for all involved. And allowing the community to help the community made our client look progressive and inclusive.

5. Respectfully correct misinformation and disinformation. Inaccurate and intentionally (or even maliciously) misleading information can be very problematic. The new admin would have to catch that sort of thing quickly and provide accurate information in a proper way.

6. Organize meet-ups. Having the admin host ad hoc meet-ups at restaurants or coffee shops while travelling for unrelated business commitments would help to humanize the admin, build stronger relationships between the organization and its community, and strengthen the community itself. Meeting people face to face would be critical to softening the tone online.

7. Listen and respond to community concerns. Hearing and acknowledging was only half the battle. The health-care organization needed to be more proactive — actually listening to its community and providing meaningful feedback.

8. Under no circumstances talk down to or at your community. That is, communicate at the same level as all members of the online community and expect to be engaged in a dialogue rather than issuing final statements on any matter. Anything that requires a change in attitude or behaviour has to be done slowly, gently, and with ample time to engage. Mark specifically said that any sudden and rash move, particularly anything done in what might be considered a sneaky way, would have disastrous effects for the client.

The client leadership were new to digital culture, making them largely uncomfortable with much of our advice. It was the last point, though, that caused them their greatest grief.

Just before shutting down for the weekend, around 4:45 p.m. on a Friday afternoon, the organization posted a letter from its leadership to their Facebook page. The essence of the letter was that the community was out of line, the organization was acting in the best interests of its community, and that the community had best be well behaved. To reinforce its role as both key-master and gatekeeper, the organization had the administrator delete a slew of critical comments from the page.

By 5:00 p.m. there were eighty extraordinarily heated comments on the page. The organization was facing the online equivalent of being drawn and quartered — all of this while the decision-makers sat blissfully unaware in rush-hour traffic. While leadership enjoyed a comfortable weekend at home, the community piled on more than two hundred additional spicy comments.

Trying to sneak something under the radar was at one time, if not an effective communication strategy, at least one that could work. And, it may still work on very rare occasion. However, trying to be sneaky is absolutely NOT worth the risk. It's far too easy for a resourceful journalist or critic to stalk and expose you ... even if you're doing the equivalent of filing permits with your municipality through a back door. Someone will notice. Someone will tweet it. Then, while you're sleeping, your critics will use their voices and organize.

Being sneaky means gambling your reputation and credibility. It's just not worth the risk.

HUMAN NEWS RELEASES

The conversation about media and social media releases is alive and well, and has been for many years. In fact, Mark was motivated to write the blog post "Social media releases: five harsh thoughts" in February 2010. After publishing that post, he found it hard to escape the discussion on the why's, how's, what's, where's and when's of using social media channels for distributing organizational information. At the time, most of the discussion revolved around text and writing style with many traditional communicators who were new to social media and felt it was acceptable to re-publish official communications written for the wire to blogs, Facebook, and LinkedIn.

Things get more interesting with the use of audio and video as a feature of the media release. We've become aware that many organizations believe adding audio and video constitutes a social media release because, as it turns out, they believe this offers the media release an interactive component. We disagree. Audio and video enrich the media release and make it easier for news organizations to include its originator in the news coverage without having to squeeze a phone call or site visit into an already tight news cycle. Multimedia content also offers the public something to share if the content is share-worthy.

Basically, we now have three types of media releases:

- traditional text-based media releases, which need to have news value and follow language and style rules (in Canada, that's typically Canadian Press style);

- enriched media releases are media releases with audio/visual components, which need to have news value and follow audio news release/video broadcast news release style rules; and,

- social media releases, which need to have appeal, offer value to the public, and provide both a platform and an opportunity for the public to engage with the publisher of the content.

THREE MEDIA RELEASES AND WHY/HOW TO USE THEM

	GOAL	TARGET	RULES	PRIMARY VALUE	MEASURE	OPPORTUNITY
MEDIA RELEASE	Communicate	Newsroom	Newsworthy & CP Style	Company/ Organization	News coverage	Finished product
ENRICHED MEDIA RELEASE	Communicate	Newsroom	Newsworthy & ANR/BNR Style	Company/ Organization/ News coverage	News coverage	Finished product
SOCIAL MEDIA RELEASE	Relationship/ Engage	Public	Good story and human voice	Public	Online conversation	Work in progress

ON THE HORIZON

Muffle Your Tweets

There are many examples of corporate Twitter accounts being host to accidentally tweeted offensive content (usually intended for the poster's personal Twitter account) or continuing to blindly post content even during a crisis or tragedy. These types of gaffes have invited widespread negative attention because Twitter makes it so damn easy for people to pile on.

Some services are looming on the horizon to help prevent that from happening to your communications department.

One, called Muffle (muffleit.com), helps organizations prevent potentially problematic tweets from being published on their Twitter account. The service keeps a database of offensive phrases or sensitive corporate information at the ready and automatically intercepts any tweets containing that content. Muffle also has a blackout function to put the account on hiatus during inappropriate times, like when a tragedy close to the brand is unfolding. Muffle can analyze the sentiment of incoming replies and retweets to provide a kind of mood monitor on the company, alerting them to potentially negative trending conversation about their brand.

Explosion of Data and the Cloud

With massive leaps in processing power and storage capability comes an unprecedented amount of data being generated. As many as five billion users could be online by 2020 — the equivalent of the entire global population in 1987. Just think how much information each person is generating simply going about their daily business — their digital trail is staggering. Is your firm prepared to process and understand the magnitude of this never-ending flow of information being created in real time?

According to a recent IBM survey, 71 percent of chief marketing officers around the world don't feel their organization is prepared to deal with the explosion of big data over the next few years, indicating that this is one of the biggest challenges for business leaders in the years to come and an area that requires a lot of attention and foresight in order to be equipped.

The cloud continues to transform how we work, play, and live. It is estimated that by 2030, virtually all work will be done in the cloud, which also will store an inexhaustible amount of data and be yet another dimension of technology-driven business. Two hundred times more data is expected to be created by 2020 than in 2008, and the cloud's storage and accessibility equals big business; in fact, the market for cloud computing will be valued at $241 billion by 2020, according to Deloitte.

Web of Things

Near field communication (NFC) technology — how smart phones and other devices in close proximity to each other exchange data — is changing the way we interact with our physical environment and each other, by transforming the world around us into a computable entity. Our homes, our cars, and even objects on the street and in our neighbourhoods will be equipped to interact with us, adding another dimension of digitalization to our physical environment.

Mobile penetration is one of the digital trends we can thank for making this futuristic vision possible, Mobile-only Internet users are slated to increase to 65 percent in 2030, and there will be an estimated 5.6 billion smart phone subscriptions by the year 2019, almost half of which will use 4G services. Mobility is critical to the progression of these advancements because so many of the interactions taking place are not happening while we're stationary in front of a computer. The other advancement that lends itself to this technology are ultralow power chips capable of harvesting energy in the environment (temperature differentials, vibrations, even radio signals), thus allowing certain devices to essentially power themselves.

Some applications, such as mobile payments and IBM's Smarter Planet initiative, a toolset using big data to advance large-scale corporate change, will become widespread in just a few years. Marketing will also be transformed, as consumers will be able to seamlessly access digital products from advertisements in the physical world.

TOUCHPOINTS: FIVE COMMUNICATIONS TAKEAWAYS

 Technology hasn't changed the need to communicate, only the parameters under which we do so. Individuals and organizations are adapting and succeeding in this new age. You can, too.

 Think before you communicate. Know what you want to achieve and recognize that's just the first step in closing in on the desired outcome. Understand what you want to say and who you want to speak to.

 It's far too easy to automate communication efforts of all forms (including pitches). Broadcasts and form letters are a surefire way to alienate your audience. Go the extra mile. Show you know who your stakeholders and interest groups are. Demonstrate you know why they matter.

 It's not always possible to have clarity in nuanced issues over certain platforms, media, or technology. It's your job to make sure your message is received. Know what you want to say, then pick the appropriate channels and wording, not the other way around.

 It's amazing how some people can make eye contact with digital audiences whether in text, images, audio, or video. Think of how you, as a person, would like to be spoken to or hear certain messages. Then deliver those messages to yourself. Others will follow.

CHAPTER 6

CUSTOMER SERVICE

Classic Plus-level children will come to the dinner table now. Prestige, Super Medallion and Executive Diamond-level children may have another five minutes of TV.

A TWEET IS NOT A CONVERSATION

It's time to inject a little honesty into the social media dialogue.

Despite grand platitudes of how Twitter is shepherding in a new era of corporate transparency and a spirit of engaging with customers, the fact remains that even the best corporate examples of such engagement on Twitter are rare at best.

Just because a company launches a Twitter account and assigns a marketing intern to issue replies to anyone who tweets at them does not mean they have engaged in any kind of conversation or dialogue. They most certainly haven't shifted any paradigms, changed any culture, moved any needles, or launched any new eras.

Social media evangelists frequently fall into the mistake of trumping up this kind of direct contact to seem like more than what it is.

A conversation is not a question answered nor a kudos thrown.

Take for example Volkswagen USA's November 12, 2013, tweet "@CinRedFed Thanks for tweeting us Cindy!" This friendly response to someone's tweet is, to be sure, a nice gesture on Volkswagen USA's part. But it's just that. A nice gesture.

Good customer service? Put down that pipe, Shaggy; it's too early to spark that bad boy.

CREATING EXPERIENCES: THE NEW SHOCK AND AWE

Like nearly everyone who owns a smart phone, we have a love-hate relationship with our own providers. Tod uses Fido. Fido's service is pretty reliable these days. Until the last year or so, the quality of their customer service was spotty at best — ranging anywhere from dismissive to apathetic. (He wants to like them, really. He's been a customer since the day they opened their doors and even sat on their advisory board for their first few years.)

For the last couple of years, their name-display service (which shows the names of inbound callers on his iPhone screen) has just never really worked. Maybe for two callers out of a hundred, the correct name will be displayed. In most cases, just the phone number appears. And yet, Fido has been charging him for this service throughout. Is this a big deal? Not so much. It's only two dollars a month. But trying to get Fido to do *anything* to take this little charge off (after all, the service doesn't work!) was like pulling teeth.

Customers Shouldn't Have to Beg

Far too many companies — and cellphone companies seem to be among the worst — operate on the principle that they'll only go as far as they're begged to by customers. And the only way the providers go above the call of duty is when competition is nipping at their heels. Canada's cellphone market is controlled by just three large companies, and, until Canada's telecommunications regulator introduced the Wireless Code in December 2013, all smartphone users had been locked into three-year contracts. The only options were to buy out the contract (expensive) or purchase a fully unlocked device (even more expensive). So Tod was stuck with Fido until December 5, 2013. In his experience, he has benefited from remarkable service in the months leading up to his contract renewal. But when he's in the thick of his contract as he is now, Fido is loathe to do much.

In this particular case, Fido blamed Apple. At one point, an Apple rep advised Tod there was no known problem like this with their phone. Not surprisingly, the rep blamed Fido. In the middle is Tod, locked to a provider who keeps billing him for name display when it doesn't work and refusing to take it off his bill until the feature is fixed.

Despite these challenges, Tod did end up renewing with Fido.

In truth — and this may come as a bit of a surprise to you — no one wireless service provider has the monopoly on good customer service. Each has their moments of heroic achievements just as they have their share of complete and utter failures.

Mark has been a Rogers mobile subscriber since the mid-nineties. What's kept him there so long? A combination of factors, really. They include the random moments of customer service glory, the dread of having to manage the logistics of changing providers, and the recognition that doing so is really just jumping from one ship to another on the same stormy sea.

When things go particularly badly with Rogers, Mark likes to point out that every time he calls Rogers, their automated phone attendant informs him that "call volume is higher than normal," presenting the question, when does higher than normal become normal?

Of greater concern is the adoption of new channels over which the same spotty level of customer service is delivered. At first blush, there's reason to be optimistic. The @RogersHelp Twitter team actively identifies and responds to customer service issues. They appear alert and responsive. However, the company's ability to deliver either online or on the phone is inconsistent at best. One particularly bad service period in the spring of 2014 saw both phone technicians and the Twitter team making commitments to call Mark back within a specified period. Months later, he was still waiting for those calls.

Delivering quality customer service must be a corporate value. Technology and empathy do not restore customer satisfaction. People do. It takes human intervention to operate technology and communicate with people in order to fix problems and make people comfortable enough to keep paying the bills.

Internet service provider (ISP) and managed hosting services company Magma Communications did this very well. Not only did they have real technicians answer the phone and stay on the line while customer concerns were solved or change requests completed, a technician would call back within a few days to make sure the customer's issue was addressed to their satisfaction and to find out if any other work was necessary. There was no upselling during the follow-up calls. That level of customer service was streamlined out of the culture when Primus bought Magma. Many customers took that opportunity to switch providers.

The Santa Clause Solution

In July 2007, a man visiting a Disney theme park was asked to leave because — are you ready for this? — he kind of looked like Santa Claus. He had a white beard and was wearing a shirt with a Santa collage. Despite a few kids asking for his autograph, it's hard to imagine he was being overtly disruptive. Despite the fact that Disney doesn't own the image of Santa (the situation might be different if the man in question came dressed head-to-toe as Mickey Claus), he claims he was asked to leave.

Could Disney have turned this into a great opportunity for everyone? Of course. They could have thanked him for coming, and handed him a bucket of free candy canes to give out. Perhaps they could have paired him with Minnie Mouse for an hour, just for fun, and gently asked him to tone it down a bit next time.

The secret to customer service is actually very simple: Surprise your customer with a proactive response and delight them with your solution.

"SURPRISE AND DELIGHT" IS THE NEW "SHOCK AND AWE" IN CUSTOMER SERVICE.

Win-Win Isn't Difficult to Achieve

Tod's solution for Fido was simple, cheap, and quick: stop charging him for name display until the thing started working.

Instead, Tod was on the receiving end of tweets and emails from Fido employees quoting replacement policies, offering excuses, and oddball metaphors. His personal favourite was as follows:

> Hi Tod.... A toaster purchased from a retailer cannot be returned two years later and an exchange requested. However, as your service provider we can go further than a toaster retailer could by offering ... to send the handset off for repair within the one-year warranty at no cost to the customer. This is how we stand by the products sold.

Tod's response?

If my toaster never cooked toast, I would expect the company who sold it to me to replace it. Wouldn't you?

Imagine if the rep offered instead: "I'm sorry that's happening. We'll take two dollars a month off your bill until name display starts working. When it does, just let us know and we'll put the fee back in place."

By doing that little bit extra and creating a situation in which they might demonstrate some trustworthiness, Tod would have absolutely returned the favour with loyalty.

How to Calculate the "Is It Really Worth It?" Factor

It boggles our minds how few companies (read: customer service reps) fail to do a simple calculation in their head — is two dollars a month (or whatever the issue is) worth pissing off a customer and the risk of losing them at the end of the contract? They're running a business, of course, so there are other factors at play, including the two most important, fiscally: How loyal has the customer been to us? And, how much money do we make from them each month currently?

Sometimes, being in customer service means making difficult decisions — maybe Fido's right and the problem originates with Apple. Is that worth a fight over two dollars?

This is of course not the fault of the customer service representative. The root cause of the problem can likely be traced back to a corporate culture which stems from the company's values. That is, the company's values need to be human-centric and embodied by its employees rather than taught, memorized, and repeated by rote?

There are many companies that empower their employees to make key customer service decisions within set parameters, without requiring permission on a case-by-case basis.

One of our favourite examples of Shock and Awe comes from Canadian pharmacy chain Shoppers Drug Mart.

One of its customers, Andrew Gardner, emailed the company to get it to stop sending inaccurately addressed mail. Jokingly, he suggested that the recipient the mail was addressed to was "a future resident of this address, and seemingly against the laws of causation, your computer system has this information and prematurely mailed an advertisement to him before he's actually lived here."

Rather than receiving the usual "Thank you for your email blah blah blah," he opened his email the next day to find this:

> Thank you for writing us. We apologize if you have been receiving mail from Shoppers Drug Mart that was addressed to another customer. Unfortunately, we cannot comment on any research projects that we may currently be conducting. However, we would appreciate it if you could provide us with some additional information that would help us determine when the mail you received was sent. Could you please let us know if it contained any of the following advertisements?

1. Now at Shoppers Drug Mart: Everexis. Cure any disease instantly with Everexis! Great for headaches, colds, cancer, and more! With no known side effects, nothing can possibly go wrong!

2. 20X The Points on Meat Products. Got the Everexis munchies? Fill your strange and unspeakable hunger and get 20X The Points!

3. 20% Off Everexis Antidote. Everexis left you slow, lumbering, and quick to anger? Take the Everexis antidote. It hasn't been fully tested, but it certainly can't make things any worse!

4. Hide in a Shoppers Drug Mart Refuge Shelter. With over 1,200 locations still standing across Canada, Shoppers Drug Mart is the ideal place to hold [sic] up and hide from the hoard [sic]. Ration Nativa Cheese Puffs and Life Brand Vitamins while you wait for rescue! Blood samples will be required for admittance.

5. Wheat, Glorious Wheat. Exclusively at Shoppers Drug Mart! Rebuild society with wheat, a traditional nonsynthetic foodstuff from the before-times. Act fast, as quantities are extremely limited.

Gardner's response? The emoticon ":0," which is generally accepted to indicate speechless surprise in text messages, emails, and other social media communications.

It turns out the response wasn't the product of a disgruntled employee. Far from it. The author was Mark Oliver — who, in addition to being happily employed by the chain for four years — also trained the email support staff and has written many of the more standard template responses used by the company.

Shoppers Drug Mart, officially, was, well, underwhelmed by Oliver's response. Company official Tammy Smitham said, "While [his] response may not have appealed to everyone, we are glad that Andrew took it in the same lighthearted way in which it was crafted. At the end of the day Andrew is a more satisfied customer (which makes us happy)."

Sometimes, creating Shock and Awe doesn't take much. Give your people the latitude to try.

Of Base Hits and Home Runs

Another way to consider Shock and Awe is through a baseball analogy.

You'll often hear baseball fans talk about how games are won. Strikeouts and home runs provide sizzle and can often determine the outcome of a game. However, most hard-core baseball fans will tell you the data shows baseball games are won by (and pardon how simple this may sound) getting players on base and then moving them around the bases to score runs.

That means walks, base hits, and bunts are an integral part of a winning strategy. Put another way, it means players must be patient and willing to be part of a team effort that recognizes wins are achieved through smaller victories. It also means individual performance statistics such as batting average and home runs tell only part of the story — the traditional glory part of the story. There are other more meaningful ways of measuring and achieving success. The tools exist for data-driven decision making. Good website analytics and online monitoring tools help determine the strengths and weaknesses of communication efforts. Analysis helps us understand what the data means and how to apply it.

OC Transpo, the public transit service in Mark's hometown of Ottawa, was on the receiving end of a significant amount of criticism from riders frustrated by schedule confusion, late buses, inconsiderate drivers, and more. The criticism came in the form of tweets, Facebook updates, and blog posts.

After some time, OC Transpo embraced Twitter as a customer service tool. They didn't make grand public pronouncements of their plans to reinvent their operations from the top down. Instead, they aimed to turn their reputation around through many small, simple acts.

It's a simple and proven technique.

OC Transpo monitored Twitter for real-time customer feedback. Then, rather than ignoring concerns or saying "noted," OC Transpo took decisive action, where possible, and responded directly with a plan of action.

The result was exchanges like this:

@SunshineC23 — Aug 1, 2012
#Octranspo 114 Hurdman @ 14:14 @ elmvale bus driver refused to lower the bus for a stroller. #Smh[14]

@OC_Transpo — Aug 3, 2012
@SunshineC23 Thanks for the feedback. We have identified the proper bus and this matter has been addressed by Transit Ops.

And this:

@Lovin_kanata — Aug 13, 2012
@Oc_transpo Time to bring bus #4423 for a check-up. The engine is shaking the entire bus. Feels like driving over rumble pad.

@OC_Transpo — Aug 13, 2012
@Lovin_kanata Thanks for the feedback. Fleet Maintenance
have been notified and will promptly address this matter.

Sometimes even tweets like this:

@Ko_bby — Aug 4, 2012
@OC_Transpo 4031 I think 176 12:15 a.m. nicest bus
driver alive[15]

@OC_Transpo — Aug 8, 2012
Thanks for the info! The operator has been ID'd and the
appropriate dept will relay the kudos on your behalf.

That's how you win ball games.

Just as base hits can win ball games, so too can some towering home runs. There are some instructive examples of organizations that send their employees to the plate with the support of the organization and the tools necessary to dazzle their customers.

The Ritz-Carlton hotel chain is a shining example of an organization with a culture of best-in-class customer service. Their employees have the authority to make decisions involving as much as two thousand dollars of company money (per incident) to address customer concerns when they occur. There's no need to put a customer on hold or ask them to wait while the front-line employee consults a superior. There's no need to extend the customer's frustration. A happy customer is a repeat customer. Often, spending a few hundred dollars to solve a problem quickly now is better than spending thousands of dollars to solve the problem later. In fact, being responsive can often cause a customer to recommit their loyalty to the company.

Author Micah Solomon tells a great story about a Southwest Airlines flight he was on that arrived at its destination late due to snow. Like many on the flight, the delay meant Solomon had missed a connecting flight and faced the prospect of joining a long queue of people fighting for the few available seats on alternative flights. As passengers walked through the Jetway toward the terminal, a Southwest employee asked for names and handed each passenger who missed their connection a ticket for the next available connecting flight. Booyah!

THE OVER-BRANDING OF COMMUNICATIONS

It was hard to hear at first, what with all the usual acoustical clutter of a busy U.S. airport, but when Tod strained to listen he was able to make it out. "We'd like to welcome our SkyLine First, StarAlliance Gold, SkyPRO Elite, and Super-Elite Passengers, Fly Higher club members, Fly Higher Gold and Silver, SuperClub, SuperClub Platinum, Diamond-Level GlobalSkies and NationalSkies members, and SunBrand Super Happy Lucky Fortune Golden Dragon passengers."

(There is a slight exaggeration at play here, of course. But not much of one.)

Ouch.

Sometimes, we wish all the airlines would get together and agree on a single, common term. Might we suggest naming these levels simply Bronze, Silver, and Gold? It worked for ParticipACTION, an initiative launched by the Canadian government in the 1970s to encourage healthy living and physical fitness among Canadians.

Stop Over-Branding

We understand why executives and branding experts prefer "SuperSkies Platinum Members" to something simpler — when you can associate a particular customer status with your own brand, it's easier to make clear the difference in service quality. If everyone called their top level "Gold," then the lousy Gold service would ruin it for the good Gold service offered by another airline.

But companies are taking it too far. And, in doing so, are making it difficult for their customers to connect with them.

Tod called his cellular service provider some time ago with a problem. To his provider's credit, their response tree had just two branches: self-service and human operator. However, that's not how the latter was identified. Fido's wording was "... or to speak to a real person using Fido Answers, press two."

Tod had no idea what Fido Answers was, but it sounded like some kind of automated system. Why couldn't the option be described as "To manage your account using your Touch-Tone keypad, press one. To speak to a real person right now, press two." Tod couldn't care any less what Fido Answers is. The very name is confusing and noncommittal.

His cable company did this too. "For Shaw Phone using Shaw Plan Personalizer, press one. For Shaw Internet using Shaw Plan Personalizer, press two. For Shaw Cablevision using Shaw Plan Personalizer, press three."

Why do companies think we care about their special little brand names for everything? We don't. We want clarity. Something like: "To order a home phone, press one. To get Internet service, press two."

COMBATTING THE LOOMING DEATH OF LOYALTY

Commit these communications errors in enough volume and you'll start losing customers. But these days, technology itself might be challenging the loyalty you hold.

Tod and his friend Patrick both do a lot of business travel. They periodically find themselves in the same city, and when they do, they try to connect for lunch.

One time they arranged to meet in the lobby of a major hotel. Patrick showed up perturbed. "Never again," he huffed. "I'm never staying here again."

Patrick was a top-level loyalty-program member of this hotel chain and he was about to switch allegiances all because of the in-room fridge. This particular hotel chain had decreased the temperature of the fridges — ostensibly to save money on energy? — and now each fridge had a sticker which basically said that while you can chill beverages fine, you probably shouldn't rely on it to keep your egg-salad sandwich at a safe temperature.

That was all it took. Patrick was willing to throw out years of loyalty because of this one simple pet peeve.

We have become an incredibly disloyal species. The membership clubs and loyalty programs of our preferred vendors' competitors lure us away more easily than before. We'll drive halfway across town because some store is offering Air Miles on purchases. It's become a huge challenge for businesses, particularly those in retail.

And it's going to get worse.

Already, mobile apps like Amazon's Price Check are popping up with the sole purpose of luring customers away from bricks-and-mortar competitors.

Here's how it works: Suppose you're looking at a kitchen mixer at a department store. You pull the box out and scan the UPC with your smart phone's camera and feed that code into Price Check. Within seconds, Amazon's database identifies the product and shows you that product at Amazon at a lesser cost. In one click.

In time, these apps will surely be merged with geo-location data, providing you with a list of retail storefront locations where you can buy that same product cheaper — within a five-minute walk.

Worse, for the retailer, this product/price-matching app is a database they *must* be in if they want to compete. Like today's business/location databases (owned by Yelp, Google, Foursquare, and others), if you're not in the app, you're losing customers.

These apps, though, come with benefits for the business owner, including the ability to run extremely time-limited offers ("Get 20% off at the till if you buy within the next 15 minutes"). To say these will be game-changers is an understatement.

Meet the Loyalty Concierge

These apps will foster an entirely new type of job — the loyalty concierge.

Look up at the ceiling of any casino and you'll see the little dark domes that hide the security cameras. Of course we all know that people are in a darkened room somewhere watching these images. But what casinos don't publicly talk about are the millions of dollars invested in guest-pattern recognition software that tracks people's movements to identify deceptive behaviour patterns.

They're the same pattern recognition techniques that pit bosses and undercover security have used for years to flesh out bad guys.

An example: Walk into a casino and loiter at a roulette table. Get really close to someone's chips. Don't play, but make lots of hand gestures near the table while you're talking. And keep looking behind your back. Your body language will alert the security pros (and that software) that you're someone they should keep a closer eye on.

Or walk in a little faster than everyone else, immediately play a single large-bet round in roulette, cash out, then walk quickly toward the exit. You might not be doing anything wrong, but your pattern is definitely worth watching.

In the very near future, we'll have loyalty concierges whose job will be, like that software, to look for cues that a customer is considering making their purchase elsewhere by browsing deals on their smart phone.

Impeccable customer service *backed by human intervention* will be the only way to get the ball back into your court.

Loss prevention officers will need to be trained to spot people using these loyalty-sniping apps much they way they're trained to sniff out shoplifters. And if they spot a potential sniping in play, they can offer items on the spot — a coupon for future purchase, a gift, free delivery, free installation for large electronics — anything that would convince someone to buy there rather than the place down the street that has it a little cheaper.

INTEGRATING MEANING THROUGHOUT THE CUSTOMER EXPERIENCE

Of course, if it were just about surprising customers with great experiences, your business probably wouldn't worry about loyalty attrition. There is, sadly, one fly in the ointment that some businesses have yet to fix — consistency of message across all platforms.

In this increasingly digital environment, companies have many customer "touchpoints," says award-winning brand strategist Craig LaRosa. "Unfortunately, the challenge is that those touchpoints may not all be connected. If they're not all telling the same story, then time, effort, energy, and resources are lost. There is an expectation that your customers should be able to come into any channel of your brand and have the same experience."

We see this dichotomy most commonly these days on brands' Facebook pages. Consider a national bank whose brand has a conservative voice. In nearly all of its marketing channels — outdoor, print, broadcast, etc. — it speaks with an air of professionalism and weight. However, its Facebook page is mostly just rebroadcasting its Twitter content, which seems to be written in the voice of an early-twenty-something keener. (Lesson: If you are a bank, you should probably avoid the use of "OMG!" in your online communications.)

> IT'S NOT THAT COMPANIES SHOULDN'T SPEAK WITH A HUMAN VOICE — THEY SHOULD, AND MUCH OF THE TRAINING AND KEYNOTE WORK WE DO IS HELPING THE MARKETING TEAMS FOR LARGE BRANDS LEARN THAT TONE — IT'S THAT YOUR COMPANY SHOULD FOREMOST SPEAK IN A CONSISTENT TONE.

Many companies structure themselves in silos of marketing, IT, sales, and operations, so there is a lack of congruency between channels.

The key, LaRosa says, is to have an overarching strategy in which each employee in every channel is working from the same playbook. That congruence must be sourced in shared passion for the company's primary mission, whether that mission is making delicious drinks or creating disruptive software.

One company that illustrates the potential success of this approach is Nordstrom.

"Nordstrom's business is built on one-to-one communication with the customer," says fashion maven Donna Karan in the book *The Nordstrom*

Way to Customer Service Excellence. "Their professional salespeople bridge the gap between the designer and the consumer." The passion for service that the book describes extends throughout the organization, from the executive offices to the shoe departments in stores to Nordstrom's online catalogue service. "They're doing a great job of connecting the experiences in the store and online," says LaRosa. "They fine-tune their in-store mix, so that if you're taking the effort to go in, you're getting something extra. Whether it's a fuller line or exclusives, they make the bricks-and-mortar store more relevant — it's not just a showroom."

In other words, it is an experience that triggers positive emotions. Visitors to Nordstrom become part of something meaningful — a passion for great customer service and respect for the profession of service provision.

The Four Seasons hotel chain has a similarly service-driven culture. Four Seasons employees make it clear that it is meaning, rather than service itself, that creates contagious fans. They receive extensive training and mentoring, whether they work in the laundry room or at the head office.

That's also true of employees of McDonald's restaurants. Tod's first job was as a "window runner" at a McDonald's at Vancouver's Expo 86 in 1986. Given that he wasn't paid much more than minimum wage, he really wasn't expecting more than an hour of training and a goofy paper hat. Instead, he ended up learning about management principles of customer service, creating emotional experiences, and even distribution channels. He certainly wasn't enrolled at the MBA level, but still — like learning how to ride a bike — Tod relies on those basic business skills to this day. By the way, he still has the goofy hat.

The difference, says one former Four Seasons employee, is a reverence for the guest. "Working at the Four Seasons is an experience I wish every young person could have," says Ingrid Craig, a former café waitress. "It was like a religion. There was simply nothing more important than the guest's experience in the hotel. We all felt like we were part of something very special, an honourable profession. At the Four Seasons, it was a privilege to serve."

Your customers can feel that sense of privilege, if it's in your employees' work ethic. Today's viral tools like Facebook can only help amplify the fruits of that ethic. Or, on the flip side, if customers sense apathy or even disdain in your staff, they'll gleefully share that online on countless consumer review sites, such as Yelp. And, like the old adage goes: You'll tell two people if you like a company. You'll tell twenty if you don't. Viral marketing can turn against you in a heartbeat.

Today, two demographic tribes with the most disposable income share similarity, says LaRosa. "The big connection between the two is their values — they are looking for meaning in their lives. In the products they buy, and their activities, they want products and experiences that feel authentic and are a reflection of their values."

A customer seeking an authentic experience when buying a product will find people who have a deep understanding of that product, he says. "They're going to find information that you just can't get anywhere else. A well-trained, articulate salesperson will provide an experience you can't get online," LaRosa explains.

"Going shopping isn't just about acquiring the thing. There's more to it than that. It's a much larger experience, whether it's education about the product or the opportunity to have a social experience with other people who are fans of the product."

When it comes to creating meaningful experiences, companies of all kinds can learn from the restaurant sector, he says. Although Apple has done an effective job of providing customers with access to "Apple Geniuses" in its stores, for example, the company has yet to leverage the quest for meaning and passion. "In their stores, they have all these Apple devotees who could talk and trade stories. They're not capitalizing on that at all," LaRosa notes.

When people go out to eat, they're seeking food, service, and ambiance, he says. "It's a total experience, and we've always looked at food this way. But more and more food offerings are going to this higher-experience, higher-touch point of view — providing more meaning. And that's where retail needs to go as well."

Otherwise, he suggests, bricks-and-mortar stores will increasingly become showrooms where customers compare products that they'll then go home and order on Amazon for ten dollars less.

In some ways, this style of shopping has been around for years. Consumers Distributing was a catalogue store that operated from 1957 to 1996. At its peak, it operated about 460 outlets. Tod remembers walking in once to get something and being greeted by a pale, lifeless, Orwellian store environment where staff served only to point you to the many catalogues scattered throughout the store and take your order. It couldn't have been less emotionally impactful. Not surprisingly, the company sought bankruptcy protection in 1996.

Today, that functionality is being carried around by your existing customers and prospects in their smart phones. And worse, any bricks-and-mortar store is at risk. Customers can walk in, scan any product's bar code with their phone's camera, and get a list of online retailers where they can get the same product cheaper. Total time: eight seconds.

So much for all your spending on brand loyalty and awareness.

DELIVERING ON THE PROMISED EXPERIENCE

There are many elements in each customer experience that may not be immediately obvious.

When someone buys a used car, for example, she may be seeking the experience of winning in the negotiation process. If the seller accepts the first price offered, the buyer may feel dissatisfied, even if the car meets her requirements and the price she pays is lower than expected.

Experienced restaurant "turnaround" experts know that a customer is used to waiting about twelve minutes for a simple meal. If a restaurant brings the food faster (which you would think would be greeted by the customer warmly), customers seem apprehensive, concerned that perhaps that item came out of the kitchen a little too fast.

If an organization's marketing communications fail to meet expectations, this may begin eroding loyalty from the first contact, and eventually do long-term brand damage, by undermining its ability to create a satisfying experience. We've all been in meetings where hours and sometimes days go by in trying to find the perfect marketing positioning statement or tagline. No matter how clever yours ends up being, it is more important that any promise your organization makes be kept when the consumer intersects with the organization.

Likewise, it's essential that everyone in the business be prepared to stand behind those promises. If a customer has to wait even a short time, or if he has to ask that a promotion be honoured, or if he isn't confident promised savings were passed along, his experience may be diminished, despite the fact that he leaves with the promised product at the promised price.

George Colombo, an expert on the use of technology in customer care, writes about what he calls the Delta Principle. According to this principle, the quality of a customer's experience is not the result of the objective quality of a company's products or services but rather stems from the congruency of the customer's expectations and the experience that is delivered.

Colombo has written about the Albertsons grocery-store chain, where one of the brand promises is low prices and employees are trained to manage customer expectations by emphasizing the savings on offer. "Instead of just putting the receipt in a bag somewhere with the groceries, the cashier takes the receipt and circles the amount of money saved by the customer with a red pen. Then, the cashier hands the receipt to the customer and says, 'You saved X dollars on your visit to Albertsons today. Thank you and please come again.'"

Ultimately, winning the digital-era war for consumer loyalty requires organizations to excel at old-school techniques — treating people well and building relationships. But even if these aims are enshrined in a company's mission statement and displayed at every workstation, translating them into measurable and strategic actions requires a deeper level of understanding.

HUMANIZING YOUR SOCIAL MEDIA

Of course, the most human type of online communication takes place over social media. That's why it's surprising that so few organizations *act* human in these spaces. They fail to embrace the "social" in "social media." Instead, they reply with boilerplate text, take far too long to respond, or don't monitor social networks for current issues or those building on the horizon.

Luckily, there are simple steps you can take to humanize your social channels.

Listen

Seek first to understand, then to be understood.
— STEPHEN R. COVEY, *THE 7 HABITS OF HIGHLY EFFECTIVE PEOPLE*

Foremost, listen. Use social monitoring tools like Hootsuite, Sprout Social, or Sysomos to monitor mentions of your brand and product names, paying close attention to questions asked and to people with high social currency (as measured by Klout or similar influence-measuring tools).

Tod's company handles the social media for many brands, including The *Vancouver Sun* Run, Canada's largest ten-kilometre race. His team, of course, keeps tabs on people commenting on the race's Facebook and Twitter channels, but more importantly the team monitors constantly active searches for specific phrases ("running" and "Vancouver") and hashtags (#RunVan is popular among local joggers). Keeping tabs on the conversation, they can jump in (speaking as the Sun Run brand) with encouraging words or a suggestion that people sign up for the run.

Many brands view social media as a one-way outbound broadcast channel. They promote products and tweet links to their own news releases without engaging their stakeholders. Sometimes, all it takes is a tweeted reply to turn people into prospects and issues into opportunities.

Face Forward

If your organization is in the business-to-consumer space, stop reading right now and go look at the avatar icon of your brand's Twitter account. If it's your logo, consider replacing it with the face of a real person.

At the Insurance Corporation of British Columbia (ICBC), which provides vehicle coverage for residents of the province, former social media head Karin Basaraba (Twitter: @K_Bas) used her real face on the company's Twitter account, providing a visual human connection to people.

"I had done a ton of research before I decided to get going with the Twitter account. I looked at other corporate accounts to see who was doing things well and who I would like to emulate. One of the accounts that I really thought was great was Scott Monty, who was running the Twitter account for Ford Motors, and I thought this would be a really great way to show the human side of ICBC. So I started using my picture as the avatar.

"We knew at the time especially that our customer perception was typical of a lot of Crown corporations: that we were bureaucratic, that we were stuffy, we put up walls, and [were] very sort of non-human. We weren't friendly or approachable and I thought, this is one way to change that perception and to show that, as a matter of fact, we are friendly and approachable."

But perhaps too approachable. With Basaraba's real face and name on the corporate Twitter account, she became the target of profanity-laden tweets sent by frustrated ICBC customers.

"When I first started, I had the gut reaction ... to ignore those — that they were just spammers or not worth my time. I remember one guy in particular who used profanity [and who] seemed genuinely frustrated, and it was at that point that I thought, nobody just tweets 'Fuck you, ICBC' on Tuesday at 2:00 p.m. without there being some reason behind it.

"So as of a bit of an experiment I started replying to every single negative tweet. It was pretty shocking to me how [negative issues] usually turned around."

Basaraba's peace-and-love missive to all haters usually resulted in one of three responses:

1. **Silence:** In most cases, the tweeters would ignore her attempts at reaching out.

2. **Bemused surprise:** People would reply and say, "LOL, I didn't realize you were actually on there listening." And sometimes: "Haha, no worries. Don't worry about it."

3. **Connection:** They would apologize for swearing (or not) but explain the issue they had or their criticism of a policy they owned.

Basaraba reflects: "I can't count the number of people that would turn around at the end and say, 'Wow. Thank you so much for helping me,' or maybe we would agree to disagree, but they were happy that I was just there to listen.

"I think that for a lot of businesses, the way they approach social media is definitely without a lot of humanity. They think of it as just an extension of their website. But I think it's a huge opportunity to extend your company's story and your company's brand.

"Really, at the end of the day, what I did at ICBC was customer service."

Basaraba also led a Twitter chat to collect feedback from ICBC customers about changes to the company's basic insurance coverage. The chat, conducted using the #askicbc hashtag, had one of its senior insurance executives answering questions and engaging with customers. This was easy to set up and provided a solid way of measuring interest in and confusion around the corporation's upcoming coverage changes.

Even if all you do is set up a web page on your site showing the faces of your forward-facing staff members, you'll go a long way toward humanizing your organization.

Use First Names

Basaraba signed her first name, Karin, to her tweets and communications in other social channels, providing another level of humanity to the mix. This practice by itself can at least partially diffuse difficult issues when people are reminded they're communicating with another human — one with feelings and thoughts of their own.

Like a growing number of organizations, each of the customer service employees working at Fido has his or her own Twitter account which they use to participate in online discussions.

Fido Eric
@FidoEric
Hi! For all your Fido Support needs, please send us a tweet
@FidoSolutions

There's just something more human about tweeting with @FidoEric than a generic @FidoCorp account.

Additionally, once your customers start talking to one specific customer service rep, they build up a relationship with them and don't have to spend as much time briefing them on an ongoing issue.

This use of first names isn't limited to Twitter accounts, of course. When your team members are engaging with members of the public, encourage them to sign their writings with their first name.

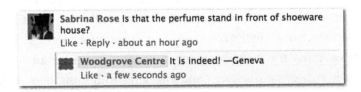

Some social media tools, like Hootsuite, provide the ability to automatically drop initials into the end of a tweet or post (the online convention is to use a caret symbol — ^ — in front). While this certainly suggests a person is behind the message and functions within space limitations, another human approach is to use a punctuation mark, like an em dash (—) in front of your first name, as in the example with Geneva, above.

On Canadian cable provider Shaw's Twitter account, customer service staff even say good night when their department closes and good morning when it reopens the next day. Even though they're using a corporate account, instead of a more personalized one like in the Fido example, reps are clear to identify themselves in their tweets either by name (see example below) or using their initials (as described above). A very human practice indeed!

> **@Shawhelp** — Jul 11, 2013
> Lance at ShawHelp saying goodnight once again. Shaw wifi hotspots are expanding across our cities! More info at ow.ly/mTdyQ!

Beware the Julies

The key is to use faces of real people who work for your organization, not just any face.

Tod once had to inquire about a specific train ticket on Amtrak, so he went to their website to try to get some information. There, on the top of the screen, was the image of a helpful customer service rep named Julie who claimed she could help.

Julie was, of course, just the brand name for Amtrak's customer service software response engine. She wasn't exactly helpful.

Typing "I need to change the seat of a wheelchair user whose ticket I have purchased" got him unrelated text about how seating is assigned. (Julie even audibly reads out the text.) Tod then typed "But I need to CHANGE the seat," and Julie, apparently suffering from brief amnesia, simply repeated back exactly what she had said before.

Don't confuse putting a human face on your Frequently Asked Questions list with actually taking steps to humanize your organization.

Julies seem to be a bit of an epidemic lately.

The Twitter account at Canadian credit union Coast Capital Savings is identified by an attractive young customer service rep named, well … guess. "Julie" responds to customer service comments online in a friendly, human tone.

> **@Coast_Capital**
> @Bradley — Hi Bradley, sorry to hear that you are unhappy. Is there anything that we can do to help?

> **@Coast_Capital**
> @Bikesandcode — Ooops is right. I'm so sorry to hear that you have had such a frustrating experience.

Good tone, to be sure.

But Julie is not a real person. Julie is just the customer-facing brand of Coast Capital. There is no real Julie. The woman in the photo was an actor hired by the company. Coast Capital's e-marketing specialist actually does most of the speaking for her, though, presumably — like "Shamu" at Seaworld, who never dies — if this real person leaves, the next person in the role will simply put on the cloak of Julie.

The idea was thought up by Coast Capital's ad agency. As head of marketing Vivian Caporale explains, it was an attempt to align off-line branches with the online service channel. "The year prior, we had introduced a new branch design. It was a very open and customer-centric design. Central to that design was the concept of having a greeter and a greeter desk. It was at the forefront of our branch design."

But when the branding team went back and looked at their website, there was a discrepancy. "That's how Julie was born. We have greeters in our branches; why don't we have greeters on our website?"

One more potential issue: Responsibility for the Julie account at Coast Capital lies with the marketing department, not the member-services department. An odd choice, considering Julie primarily deals with members' inquiries and complaints. It's reminiscent of the days when the IT department held a tight rein on a company's forward-facing website — technically, yes, it's an information technology product, but its real value was marketing the organization. While certainly tight integration is necessary between the two teams (after all, Caporale notes, "there's a certain level of quirkiness and humour that really talks about our brand personality"), the main department holding responsibility for member services should be, well, member services.

While some would argue that the Julieization of the Web at Coast Capital puts a humanizing face on the organization's support team, members will soon realize that the person they've been talking to all along wasn't who they thought. It's a good start, but this particular implementation of humanizing their member services department goes only halfway.

To be fair, Coast Capital's Julie account does indeed provide stellar service. Most tweets — even angry ones from members — are responded to in a personable tone. And with more than a half million members (making them Canada's largest credit union by membership) and fifty branches in southwest British Columbia, they're clearly doing something right. We'd like to see them use real people in their dealings with real members.

BUILDING A HUMAN-BASED SUPPORT CENTRE

One of the most important components of an organization's customer service is its support centre. These days, service reps handle phone calls, email, live chat sessions, and social media.

Here are some recommendations we have for building a more human support centre.

Email

It was supposed to be the solution to easing customer support — let people email a generic support@ email address and have software route the inquiry to the right person. Backed by software, theoretically this should keep conversations with a single rep who has the history of the issue at hand.

Sadly, these email support tools haven't evolved much, and we're stuck with the "Reply Above This Line" threads which sometimes seem endless, riddled with canned responses. It seems increasingly like support people don't read the emails much at all — instead they seem to glance at an email, find a few keywords, and match it to a canned response they have.

Here's an exchange Tod had with NetNation, the domain provider he once used.

NetNation's original email, 2:24 a.m.:

> The service(s) listed below are about to expire and require your immediate attention. You must renew or your service(s) will be deactivated upon expiration. Your service(s) and possibly your business will be interrupted. Domain: *thirdtuesdayvancouver.com.*

Tod's response, 11:19 a.m.:

> I would like to renew this, but when I go to account manager (following your link) it doesn't show me that domain. Help! I do not want this domain deleted.

Netnation's "response," 11:48 a.m.:

> We received a request that you no longer wanted this domain, so it was closed, and autorenew was removed. If this is no longer the case, please provide us with the

last four characters of your account manager password,
and we will reopen it, to enable renewal of the domain.

What? That's not at all what Tod had asked. In fact, Tod asked for quite the opposite.

There's nothing wrong with having pre-approved templates to guide your reps, but a human organization will use these templates as direction pointers, not as actual texts.

Encourage your support team to translate the template text into something personal and directly relevant to a given inquiry.

We like customer support software provider SupportBee. It doesn't use Reply Above This Line or other miscellaneous administrivia (really, do your customers care what time the agent replied in the UTC time zone?). Correspondence shows up as a regular email between two regular people.

Better yet, an emotion-gathering question might help prioritize the inquiry, beyond the usual staid "Low, Medium, High."

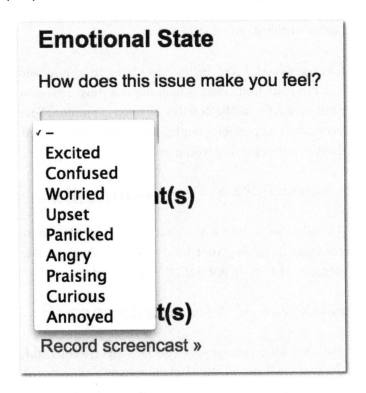

Telephone

Likewise, phone support lines seem to have their own non-human jargon. Think about how much time in a month you spend listening to corporate "please hold" messages. It's gotten to the point that most of us can guess what the recorded voice is going to say before we're plopped into the queue.

When you think about it, many of these statements can be dismissed as outrageous.

Consider these examples and excise them from your phone-tree system if your organization uses them.

"WE ARE EXPERIENCING A HIGHER-THAN-AVERAGE CALL VOLUME."

No, you're not. (We're looking at you, Shaw Cable. You've had that on your please-hold message since 1821.) In most cases, it's not that the organization is suddenly experiencing more calls, it's that they've chosen to not add more staff. Really — did suddenly — just before your customer called on Tuesday at 11:20 a.m. — hundreds of people flood your call centre to discuss something?

Some companies even have the audacity to take this one level further with ...

"BECAUSE OF OVERWHELMING DEMAND FOR OUR PRODUCT, WE'RE EXPERIENCING ..."

This isn't the time to brag. Answer the phone.

"OUR MENU OPTIONS HAVE CHANGED."

Stop it. They haven't and you know it. Companies use this line because they want to rope people into listening to their whole spiel first — which often includes product ads. Menu options don't change often. Even if they do, do you really have to leave that on your message for the next five years?

"SO THAT WE CAN ROUTE THIS CALL TO THE RIGHT AGENT, PLEASE CHOOSE FROM ONE OF THE FOLLOWING OPTIONS."

This is one of the oldest tricks in the books. It's called the "operator 123" trick in marketing circles. You know those ads that say to call their number and ask to speak to operator 123? Of course, there is no operator 123. That was ad number 123 you just responded to, and by asking for a specific operator, you've helped them track which ad it was.

That's basically what's happening with many of these corporate please-hold messages. You're going to talk to the same operator no matter which button you push. What you've done instead is logged a little reference in some tracking database about what product you own or what your complaint is. And then, you simply get pawned off on whichever agent comes up next.

"YOUR CALL IS IMPORTANT TO US."

The paradox here is that the companies who dole out this rote, weak statement, are the ones who seem to care the least about their customers — at least judging from their customer service. Really — how do they know the next call is going to be important to them? Maybe the caller will just yodel for the first thirty seconds. That's not going to be so important. Drop the line. It's unnecessary.

We recommend Laura Penny's book *Your Call Is Important to Us: The Truth About Bullshit.*

"PLEASE CHOOSE FROM ONE OF THE FOLLOWING OPTIONS."

This would be great if the options they're offering had anything to do with why you were calling. As Tod was writing this book, his financial institution called him seven times in the space of an hour. He was on an important call at the time and let the bank's calls go to voice mail. Since there were so many calls in the space of such a short time, he wondered if there was something wrong. So he called their number.

Now remember, he is calling to ask why they called and if it was important. Which option would you pick?

1. Check your balance, pay a bill, transfer funds, or change your personal access code

2. Branch information or phone directory

3. Loans, mortgages, or lines of credit

4. Information on new tax-free savings account or other investments and rates

5. Visa questions, including lost and stolen cards

6. Personal or business banking needs

He guessed six, only because it was the most generic. Of course, it was the last option offered.

Which brings us to perhaps the most outrageous statement of them all.

"THIS CALL MAY BE RECORDED FOR QUALITY ASSURANCE PURPOSES."
You're offering better service because a hard disk somewhere is recording the conversation? Get real. Of course, if the call goes weird, you might be able to use it to train future reps on how to handle problem calls, but the fact that you're recording the call doesn't help your customer get anything.

Many people believe this exists because of legalities — that you must tell someone you're recording a call if you are. Fact is, across all of Canada and most American states there is no such obligation.

Sadly, there are fewer and fewer companies that offer a more human approach as simple as this:

"You've reached the customer support line of ABC Widgets. Please hold for an operator."

Would that be so hard?

Live Chat
One of the worst implementations of customer service online are web-chat applications where users type comments to a live representative in a chat pop-up web browser box.

Managers often become enamoured of these tools because they are trackable (all conversation is logged for future review), pre-approved template-based replies can be easily pasted in, and a rep can theoretically carry on more than one conversation at a time.

The problem is, in practice this is a lousy approach which ends up frustrating users more than helping them. Here are some tactics to ensure the humanity isn't lost if you must use these tools.

CAP THE MAXIMUM CONCURRENT CONVERSATIONS AT THREE.

With one rep trying to talk to ten people at the same time, there are often long delays. The user sits waiting for a basic reply for several minutes at a time — sometimes having to prompt the rep with a "Hello? Are you still there?"

Don't kid yourself. Users are smart. They can tell when they're just one of many chat windows on the rep's screen.

DON'T RELY ON COPY AND PASTE.

Far too many of these conversations end up being little more than quick copy-and-paste jobs. The worst offender is the "I am happy to help and can definitely assist you with this" line — which, more times than not, is followed by the representative admitting they can't actually help the user.

Or after short sentence responses, suddenly the rep dumps in a pre-approved template response like "Thank you again for the opportunity to have served you. If you need more assistance, please visit our website. The system will now prompt you to rate the quality of this service."

It's robotic and not human.

Of course you should have consistent messaging. However, it's just as important, perhaps more so, to encourage your reps to use their own words for these common questions or responses.

ENSURE YOUR TEAM SPEAKS ENGLISH. WELL.

It seems that many of these chat-based systems are used by call centres in developing nations where English is often not the rep's first language. This can result in confusion and frustration on both the rep's and the user's end. Using chat systems is not a substitute for good communication.

PROVIDE A PHONE LINK.

Some issues are just too detailed to type in one word at a time. Either they're quite technical or there's a lengthy background that needs more explanation. Forcing people to type this in is insulting. Instead, provide a way for users to call in to the specific rep they're currently chatting with — a direct number or extension, so the background isn't lost and there's no need to spend more time briefing a new agent.

Your rep should offer this phone-in (or phone-out) ability at the start of the session. Consider the second question all Apple customer service reps ask (after your first name): "Is there a number I can reach you at in case we get disconnected?"

Remember: Your goal is to help in the most effective and quickest way possible.

To be fair, some of these tools are getting better with age. LivePerson can pop up proactive "Can I help?" boxes when people land on specific web pages, like pricing pages. The icon might be a photo of a specific agent, and sometimes you can deploy video inside the chat box. (This small tactic really increases the human connection.) And the system permits reps to transfer the chat to someone else internally.

ON THE HORIZON

Listening for Human Emotion

Have you ever heard the urban legend that swearing loudly at an automated phone tree (Robot: "Please tell me what product you're calling about." Caller: "SCREW YOU! GET ME A HUMAN REP!") can move you to the start of the call queue?[16]

Soon, your customer support centre might be able to help prioritize callers based just on their current state of emotion.

A platform called Beyond Verbal analyzes vocal intonations in order to understand what emotions people are feeling as they speak. Backed by nearly twenty years of research, the system records voice and breaks it down into fifteen-second chunks, then analyzes the vocal intonation of each chunk. The system can spit out a score or coding system that software developers can plug into to change the status of a call instantly.

Besides the obvious application in a call centre, the developers believe their tool will take root in online dating services, political "truth-seeking," and other applications.

Although to be fair, when Tod tested the mobile-app emotion detector on an otherwise happy day, it registered his state of emotion as "unhappy — pain, vulnerable, need to fight."

Regardless, remember: Words alone don't always tell the human story.

Direct to Rep

Phone trees (press one for this, press two for that) are the bane of all of our lives. One firm, Israel-based Zappix, has found a more elegant and human solution.

Zappix substitutes voice-tree menus with a smart phone-app that prompts the caller to select the right department on a web page before they even make the call. Once they've made their selection it's saved in the app so they can dial up the right extension without having to go through the tree again. Callers can connect to the right rep up to 90 percent faster without having to rely on your organization's existing set-up. A management panel lets you change these options in real time as needed.

The app is free and works on iPhone and Android devices.

Live Response Time

This might frighten you if your customer service response time is slow, but airline KLM posts its live Twitter response times right on its Twitter account.

"We believe in the transparency of social media," KLM Senior Vice-President Martijn van der Zee says. "Customers want to know what to expect from us."

This is done through the surprisingly low-tech method of updating KLM's Twitter cover photo every five minutes, showing the current wait time for a Twitter response in the image.

TOUCHPOINTS: FIVE CUSTOMER SERVICE TAKEAWAYS

 Technology offers new and powerful ways to identify customer service opportunities and issues, and to make informed decisions. However, interacting through a piece of glass can make things impersonal. Never before has there been a stronger argument against corporate-speak and legalese.

 Customers are happy when they get the product or service they were expecting from their purchase, their problems addressed quickly and with the least amount of friction, and they feel heard. Keeping customers happy is an organizational commitment.

 Doing something out of the ordinary can certainly get attention. However, like in a marriage or friendship, loyalty and trust grow through routine efforts. Sometimes being unique means taking care of the little stuff.

 Nothing sends a mixed message to customers quite like unpredictable service or service tied to contract renewal cycles. Clarity is more than just saying what you'll do and doing it. It also means being consistent.

 Customers like to know they have been heard and understood, and they like to be spoken to (not at) in language that resonates with them. No amount of technology in the world will ever replace the value of human intervention.

CHAPTER 7

MARKETING

I look at this, and it fills me with hope
that there's some way to monetize it.

I make movies for the masses, but I talk to them one at a time.
— STEVEN SPIELBERG

THE RECIPE FOR CONTAGIOUS LOYALTY

You wouldn't think so by looking at it, but the idea for Vancouver's popular Juice Truck street-food truck was actually conceived in a tiny, high-altitude village in Nepal. Stranded in the village by snow as they trekked in the region, Zach Berman and Ryan Slater learned that the villagers took in many of their vital nutrients from a bright orange drink made from sea buckthorn berries. Passionate about health, the two young men began daydreaming about opening a juice bar that served great-tasting, high-nutrient drinks. As their travels continued, they visited juice bars around the world, collecting recipes and comparing processes.

By the time Vancouver's municipal government announced its aim to make Vancouver a street-food-friendly city, Berman and Slater had transformed their passion and recipes into a business model. They bought and refurbished a 1980s Grumman Kurbmaster truck, installed a pricey cold-press juicing machine proven to extract the highest volume of nutrients, committed to using organic, locally grown produce, and set up shop in Vancouver's trendy Gastown. Less than a year later, their customers are not just regulars but "contagious" loyal fans. Why?

Let's break it down in management theory terms. A business gains loyalty when it has a brand that resonates with an audience, provides excellent customer service, uses competent marketing, and deploys quality control and effective relationship management. You don't need to go to MBA school to learn those essentials.

But that theory misses the essence of loyalty, says Jesse James Garrett, director of user experience strategy for Adaptive Path, a design firm based in San Francisco. "Positive experiences create the emotional bonds that lead to customer loyalty," he says. In other words, each of these elements is successful only to the degree that it contributes to the quality of the overall customer experience.

It turns out, in many ways, marketers have been getting it wrong all along. The foundation of loyalty is not reason, but human emotion.

The Search for Meaning

According to the authors of *Firms of Endearment*, the foundation of loyalty is the creation of a particular set of emotions that can be described as "meaning." As backed by numerous consumer surveys, your consumers are looking for higher meaning in their lives, rather than simply adding to their store of belongings. The companies that succeed in this environment are those that ask the question "How are we going to make this company an instrument of service to society, even as we fulfill our obligation to create shareholder wealth?"

The authors — Dr. Jagdish Sheth, world-recognized authority on global competition, strategic thinking, and customer relationship management; David Wolfe, internationally recognized customer behaviour expert; and Rajendra Sisodia, professor of marketing and founding director of the Center for Marketing Technology at Bentley University — go so far as to predict that companies "without a soul" have a doubtful future. They contrast Wal-Mart's stagnant stock value with Target's 150-percent increase over five years as an example. Wal-Mart provides low prices; Target's customers enjoy low prices, high style, and a pleasant shopping experience. It's the difference between a customer and a contagious fan.

So, let's deconstruct the Juice Truck experiences of Liz, a regular customer and brand advocate, to examine how this search for meaning might apply to her loyalty to this small business.

It was only a matter of time before this fervent foodie and trend-spotter found a favourite street-food vendor, if only to be part of the culture. Always looking for pleasurable ways to increase her nutrient intake, when she spotted the Juice Truck in her neighbourhood, she stopped by for The Classic, a juice made of apple pressed with carrot, beet, and ginger.

Though the Juice Truck is mobile, for the hipsters working in the many local technology and social media–strategy companies, tourists, and Vancouver residents with an appreciation of Gastown's heritage buildings, its regular spot is a prime location. Just off cobblestoned Water Street, the big pink truck shares the block with an artisanal barbershop, shoemaker, and local fashion designer, as well as one of Vancouver's most popular pubs and three of the city's hottest restaurants.

Here's the way another fan, Robin, describes the Juice Truck experience on Yelp: "They do local, seasonal, fresh fruits and veggies ... all blended or cold-pressed to make a perfectly refreshing and energy-inducing drink. And really, could they be any cuter? Super passionate about their product, and genuinely happy to be a local business, these two make it easy for me to fork over a few extra bills to buy a drink."

In other words, everything about the experience of buying at the Juice Truck is congruent with the company's mission, and being part of that experience is worth paying more.

Back to Liz: While waiting for her juice, she used her smart phone to start following the Juice Truck on Twitter, thinking it might be useful to hear about their specials. As the person serving her seemed friendly, she shared that she worked at home and needs reasons to get out of her apartment on a more regular basis. He promised to try to entice her with delicious specials. A few days later, when she saw a tweet advising that the afternoon special was hot chocolate made from small-batch, ethically sourced, locally produced Beta5 chocolate, Liz put down her laptop and headed out.

The chocolate drink is made by heating almond milk to a precise temperature and pouring it over handmade, bourbon-smoked marsh-mallows. Dipping a solid block of organic Beta5 dark chocolate–on-a-stick into the mixture, he reverently handed it to Liz and told her to wait for about two minutes and then stir. Obediently, feeling almost as if she was participating in a kind of sacred rite, she followed the directions precisely, and then took her treasure back to her home office.

And that's when Liz went from being a satisfied customer to becoming a contagious fan — an active advocate for Juice Truck.

The drink was so memorable that she immediately tweeted her appreciation; later that day, before they packed up the truck, one of the Juice Truck staff retweeted her message, along with their thanks. That weekend, when the conversation turned to food at a party, Liz mesmerized her friends with a description of the hot chocolate–making process and the mobile juice bar. Within three weeks, four of the people that heard her story had all become Juice Truck customers and advocates.

Liz's Juice Truck experience demonstrates the power of cultivating contagious passion in your customers. Facebook CEO Mark Zuckerberg and Microsoft's Bill Gates famously dropped out of Harvard to focus on building the technologies they were passionate about; Apple's Steve Jobs's passion for style and design is legendary. Not all businesses are founded in passion, but those that thrive find a way to create a passionate culture, to instill a high level of passion in their employees, and through their employees, to enable their customers to share in that passion through meaningful experiences. And that is the recipe for both a great juice and a raving fan, ready to spread news about your brand.

CONNECTIONS AND BIOCHEMICAL REACTIONS

An ad was played in movie theatres as part of the pre-feature entertainment we've come to accept. Mark's family saw the ad when they went to see *Brave*, a Pixar offering, on his youngest daughter's birthday.

The ad featured a series of visuals and assertions about what makes Canada great. The visuals included the Canadarm, the building of the railway, snow-capped mountains, a horse plough team, the building of the CN Tower, and more. Each visual was accompanied by statements like "When faced with adversity, Canadians look for a way, not a way out." It was in the genre of Apple's 1997 "Here's to the Crazy Ones" ad. The theatre audience was riveted. You could have heard a pin drop.

Then, something jarring happened that yanked the entire theatre out of that inspired moment.

The inspiration turned into a blunt sales pitch; inspiration became propaganda. The beautiful archives and stock footage became computer imagery. And, when presented with the narration, "So, when no one thought it was possible to unlock the potential in the oil sands ..." a large portion of the audience broke out laughing. Others moaned.

It turned out the second half of the ad systematically undid everything the first half did so well. The ad went from sharing an inspired moment with Canadians to spewing talking points at the now-trapped audience.

The concept of the ad was brilliant. The execution was a disaster. The comments posted to the video on YouTube reflect that.

YOUTUBE COMMENT

This thing is so classic, you don't even see it coming. When we saw this in the theatre and it started on the oil sands we started laughing so hard.

— MrGaru2xx

Consider the established masters of inspiring ads. Apple and Nike know how to inspire people and to sell products without a sales pitch. They explore an idea people want to be a part of and simply attach their name to it. They remind us of our individual potential and that what each of us does matters — and they do it in a way that suggests that what they do matters too. They sell the idea, not the product or the company. The product sells itself. The company earns respect.

Apple and Nike succeed because they show us why we matter. They remind us of our human potential and, in doing so, associate themselves with human potential. They identify themselves as our cheerleaders. They speak human. More importantly, they know when to stop speaking.

Modern marketing has changed a lot. Many people in the C-Suite of established enterprises, those with long-standing traditions of doing business a certain way, still think public opinion is swayed and sales made by pushing product. They haven't caught up with modernized values which sell the benefit.

Cenovus Energy, creators of the oil sands ad, missed a perfect opportunity to cut to its logo at the thirty-second mark. For added effect, they might have put a memorable website address on the screen.

Even better, Cenovus might have simply provided a link to a website URL suggesting Canadian innovation without any branding in the ad. Members of the inspired audience would surely want to find out more. The destination could be a microsite which would deliver a blended message of Canadian innovation, human potential, and oil sands achievements.

The public is no longer interested in corporate-speak, legally vetted messaging, and homogenized statements. Companies need to recognize they are competing for public attention with all industries, not just their own. Whether trying to win in the court of public opinion, recruiting, or just hoping to earn some general consideration, the C-Suite needs to give the public a reason to see them differently on the public's terms.

THE MARKETING-BY-ADVERTISING SHIP SAILED LONG AGO. IT HAS BEEN REPLACED BY MARKETING BY ENTERTAINMENT AND THE MORE EFFECTIVE MARKETING BY INSPIRATION.

Red Bull knows this very well. They've proven to be a media company that happens to sell an energy drink, rather than an energy drink company that inspires people through its ambitious sponsorship of human potential.

They're known for sponsoring extreme sporting events, including wakeboarding, cliff diving, and aerobatic races. The sponsorships create opportunities to generate incredible, high-quality multimedia content which captures and triggers the chemical reaction of adrenalin from engaging in and witnessing incredible feats.

Perhaps the best known Red Bull sponsorship was the Red Bull Stratos project. The extraordinarily ambitious and dangerous dream of daredevil Felix Baumgartner, Red Bull Stratos innovated new technology that made it possible for Baumgartner to be hoisted to the edge of space, where he stepped off the ledge of his space capsule and began a thirty-nine-mile skydive. On October 14, 2012, protected only by a spacesuit, Baumgartner became the first person to break the sound barrier without a rocket before gently (and triumphantly) landing on the ground.

More than eight million people around the world watched the live stream. To the audience, most of the three-hour ascent was dull and uneventful. The descent was heart-stopping. It took nine minutes and nine seconds.

The planning and preparation took seven years. The story of the project, from conception to the studying of the post-jump data, is told in *Mission to the Edge of Space: The Inside Story of Red Bull Stratos*, a two-hour documentary released one year after the jump.

The energy drink was incidental to this sensational feat. And Red Bull's name is forever attached to space and aeronautic research.

How important is high-quality content to the Red Bull brand? The existence of Red Bull Media House says it all. These talented and well-equipped content producers create remarkable broadcast media, movies, videos, print material (including magazines), games, mobile apps, websites, and music. And, they're phenomenal storytellers, which speaks to their ability to achieve TOUCH.

It's interesting how the Super Bowl has become more than a faceoff between the two most accomplished football teams of the National Football League. It has become a pageant of some of the best, fresh brand advertising, perhaps because of Apple's legendary "1984" Super Bowl ad aligning Apple with counterculture, directed by Ridley Scott.

Seattle Seahawk running back Derrick Coleman was the subject of the captivating "Trust Your Power" ad created for the 2014 Super Bowl. In the sixty-second spot, Coleman tells of his overcoming the challenges of being deaf since age three to make it to the annual football championship. He tells of being picked last in schoolyard and professional drafts, punctuated by familiar visuals of the pain associated with being left behind. Another sequence shows a young football player digging through the dirt of a football field to recover a hearing aid knocked out during a tackle, followed by a shot of the player taping his ears down with medical tape to hold his hearing aids in place for a subsequent game. Audio processing suggests the challenges of being hard of hearing while receiving instructions yelled at you by a coach in the chaos of a game.

The ad is inspiring. As a viewer, you can't help but relate to the feeling of facing insurmountable challenges and disappointments. You may feel a little ashamed that you did so with the full operation of all of your senses. Most importantly, you feel energized as Coleman's story takes a positive turn. You might feel you are part of the victorious climax when Coleman announces, in reference to the Super Bowl, "Now I'm here with the loudest fans in the NFL cheering me on. And I can hear them all."

"Trust Your Power" was posted to YouTube[17] on January 10, 2014. By the time of the Super Bowl XLVIII coin toss sixteen days later, eleven million people had watched the ad. With its suitably chosen double-entendre title, this inspiring short documentary is Duracell's contribution to the pageant. But that information isn't available in the clip until fifty-seven seconds has passed — 95 percent of the way through ad. That's when a Duracell battery appears on the screen along with the familiar musical triad, the visual and audio branding.

Think of all the battery commercials you've seen over the past thirty years. How many sell the product? How many sell the function? What kind of biochemical reaction did you naturally experience when you watched those ads? How likely were you to watch any of them more than once? How many were you likely to share with your family, friends, and colleagues?

Now, how many battery commercials have connected you with human achievement supported by a battery? What kind of biochemical reaction did you naturally experience when you watched those ads? How likely were you to watch any of those ads more than once? How many were you likely to share with your family, friends, and colleagues on Facebook, Twitter, LinkedIn, through email, or even in a conversation about cool things you saw online?

In many ways, "Trust Your Power" is reminiscent of an old thirty-second Nike spot featuring Michael Jordan. In the 1997 ad, Jordan, basketball's most celebrated player of the day, solemnly details a career full of failures — number of games lost, missed shots, and missed game-winning shots he was trusted by his team to make. The ad closes with Jordan declaring, "I have failed over and over and over again in my life, and that is why I succeed."

This is a message that resonates with people. It's very TOUCH. This is why so many companies are embracing marketing by inspiration. They're turning their attention to a digital culture hungry for connection to human potential. If they succeed, the audience will do the amplification for them. This puts the onus on companies to direct their efforts at establishing a more interactive, more meaningful connection with their audiences. And, in the spirit of Michael Jordan's statement, companies are allowed to fail so long as they publicly learn from their failures and use them to succeed.

Oreo scored a big TOUCHdown during the 2013 Super Bowl (please excuse the pun). The power went out in half of the Superdome in New Orleans during the championship football game. The lights remained off for thirty-four minutes. Proving that they were paying attention and were creative, the Oreo team jumped on the opportunity and issued a tweet with the words "Power out? No problem," featuring an image of a lone Oreo cookie against a white-to-black gradient background and the words "You can still dunk in the dark."

The tweet wasn't just creative; it was timely. Its appeal to restless football fans was unmistakable, earning ten thousand retweets in the first hour after it was issued and a significant amount of mainstream media attention.

This simple tweet was pure genius and became the talk of Super Bowl marketing that year. It still gets mentioned and analyzed in many digital marketing conversations (and in some books) because of the shared media and earned media attention it gained. In fact, some argue (and we agree) this simple tweet likely had a better payoff for Oreo than their television ad for the event. The ad likely came with a multimillion-dollar price tag. In stark contrast, the tweet probably cost a few thousand dollars of creative time and approvals, all of which reportedly came together in minutes, involving people watching the game in the same room. Score a victory for Oreo and its creative agency, 360i.

Pepsi took a different approach in 2010. That was the year the food and beverage company reallocated the twenty million dollars it would have spent on a commercial during the Super Bowl to the Pepsi Refresh Project, an initiative to fund projects hoping to achieve a positive impact on communities and the world at large. Individuals and organizations were invited to propose ideas which were then made available for online voting. The most popular ideas each month were awarded grants worth anywhere between five thousand and two hundred fifty thousand dollars.

While not without its problems, this altruistic campaign was very effective. It afforded Pepsi a greater amount of positive attention than the company would have received from a clever and creative thirty-second spot. Plus, because the program stretched over twelve months, the earned media attention and positive online mentions paid off in spades.

Like many companies, Pepsi is approaching their human-digital strategy from multiple fronts. One example comes from Pepsi Netherlands. Working with creative agency LikeFriends, they bought a 1966 Dodge A100 van and made it the central character in an interactive and engaged Facebook community. They called it the Pepsi Rider. It was wrapped and given as a gift to their Facebook community. A fan responded to an invitation to publically unwrap the van, an event that was captured on video.

Since then, members of the exclusive online community (membership criterion is that you have to respond to updates) are co-creating the life of the Pepsi Rider through a custom-built app. They've suggested paint jobs and interior decorations and travel destinations, all of which have been voted on for final decisions. The winning paint job was applied by the fan whose design was selected.

The van really has become a character. Fans follow online and have opportunities to see the van in action. They've seen videos hosted by Harold, the energetic caretaker/driver of the van; fans navigating the Pepsi Rider through an obstacle course; delivering it to events; and having it outfitted with a sound system and speaker array. The Pepsi team has also posted photos of Harold leaning out of the driver's window with a stack of pizza boxes, offering to deliver Pepsi and pizzas to anyone moving on a particular weekend. They've also posted pictures of the van on a flatbed tow truck after breaking down during a road trip.

The Pepsi Rider is fun, edgy, and interactive. It gives fans the opportunity to feel as though they play a deeper role with Pepsi than being mere consumers of beverages and snacks. They're part of a brand that's hip. They're made to feel as though they're collective participants in a real-life game. Moves don't happen unless they help make it so. It's not about Pepsi. It's not about buying and drinking Pepsi. It's about fun and doing outrageous things to an aging vehicle. It's about young people engaging in young fun. Brought to you by Pepsi.

And, if you're one of those people who measures Facebook success by the number of people who like a page, in January 2014 there were more than thirty-one million likes of Pepsi Netherland's fan page. Incidentally, there were also more than two hundred thousand people talking about the page.

The biggest story on human connection from 2013 might be WestJet's "Christmas Miracle: Real-Time Giving" video. Posted to YouTube on December 8, 2013, the video had over thirty-five million views by the end of January 2014.

In case you haven't seen it, the video documents an elaborate and very clever scheme. Television screens set up in each of two airport terminals (Toronto and Hamilton, Ontario) allowed passengers of two specific flights to interact with an actor dressed as Santa Claus after scanning their boarding pass. Passengers registered their gift wishes with Santa, whose elves (WestJet employees) recorded them. While the planes were in flight, WestJet employees bought the requested gifts, wrapped them, and tagged them for their intended recipients.

After arriving at their destinations, the same unsuspecting passengers who had spoken with Santa watched as gift after gift spilled down the conveyor belt to the baggage carousel.

The entire event is masterfully shown in the video. It has all the magic and excitement of Christmas, combined with the energy and pressure of shopping and wrapping to deliver the gifts against the clock. From the setting-up of the video screens in the terminals, to the shocked and emotional faces of the passengers as they opened their gifts — from underwear and socks to large-screen televisions and diamond rings (delivered by Santa on bent knee) — the entire event was captured for all to see.

How expensive was that campaign? Who cares? The social media attention it received drove international media attention. That might be payoff enough since we personally know people who have declared WestJet is now top of mind when making North American travel plans. However, there is an even bigger payoff. By all accounts, the campaign had a significant motivational aspect on the WestJet organization. Employees contributed the idea. Employees executed the idea. Employees saw the public response to their campaign. And, employees saw the impact the campaign had in reports in mainstream media. The campaign to give to others also turned into the organization giving to itself. How human is that?

BRIDGING BIG DATA AND EMOTION

Big data has become quite the buzzword of late. Really, big data is data as it has always been — information gathered which reveals demographics, psychographics, usage patterns, purchase decisions, voter intention, etc. — just lots of it.

Technology has made it possible to track consumer behaviour and measure responses to campaigns. This allows us to make informed decisions on how to prepare messages within character constraints, the best colours and fonts choices for a web page, the right call to action, and the right app functionality to engage the public. For the most part, collecting this information is free, or at least fairly cheap. The real cost comes in analyzing the data. Regardless, there's really no excuse to not reap the benefits of gathering and analyzing data.

Google Analytics, YouTube Statistics, Facebook Insights, and social media monitoring and measurement tools such as Sysomos MAP and Sysomos Heartbeat need to be in your tool box.

Competition for public attention is fierce. You're no longer just up against a competitor's YouTube videos. Your audience is being redirected to news reports of Justin Bieber's latest indiscretions, tweets about Toronto mayor Rob Ford's most recent crude remarks, and Facebook updates featuring infographics on the latest social media trends. If you're not using every bit of data available to understand who your target audience is and where it's gathering, you may have already lost.

Data is just the raw material, though. You need to parse through the data to find the people and stories within. It's a bit like paleontology. Two adjacent pieces of data might be closely connected. However, it's just as likely you'll need data from multiple sources to truly understand what you're looking at.

Then, just like a paleontologist, you need to mix and match the data to determine how it interrelates and what the human element is within the data. Then you can work from a better place.

The good news is, technology is advancing at a tremendous pace. We're figuring out how to automate nearly everything. Computers can buy stocks, sell books, refund purchases, and more. In many cases, they're better at it than we are. They're faster, make fewer errors, and do it more cheaply. Plus, they don't take weekends off to catch up with the family.

But there are at least two advantages humans still have over automated systems — intuition and emotion. We make purchase decisions based on our emotions and feelings all the time. If you don't believe us, watch any television ad for a luxury car and listen to the narration. It's not talking about the speed of the on-board microchips. It's speaking to the human element in each of us — the desire to feel pampered, to boast about our successes to our friends, and so on.

So far, the best approach marketers have come up with to marry the two (technology and emotion) is to imply you'll feel better after buying their product.

But what if technology could identify human emotion and use that to market more effectively? It turns out, that's possible today — though few brands are capitalizing on it.

Imagine you run a hotel where one of the profit lines is timeshare sales. How would you have identified likely purchase candidates previously? You might have put a desk in the lobby, looked for people who appeared to be married, and offered them tickets to a show and dinner in exchange for ninety minutes of their time to go through a hard-sell pitch.

A more human approach would be to exploit biometrics to identify people already likely to buy. You'd simply scan the lobby for people who are giving off biometric signals (skin temperature and facial expression recognition being the two primary biometric metrics today) that meet the emotional profile which is most optimal for your selling.

In the case of this hotel timeshare example, you'd be looking for people who are relaxed, curious, happy, or bored.

Of course this kind of technology is not just limited to facial skin temperature or micro expressions, it's also pattern recognition — *how* someone walks through the lobby. We'll get to that in a moment.

Cued Retrospective Recall

The technology that will bridge big data with emotion can do other things as well — such as monitor the human decision-making processes inside a bricks-and-mortar store.

BYE BYE RED EYE

When Dutch coffee manufacturer Douwe Egberts wanted to promote its product, it realized that people were more likely to consider buying coffee when they were tired. The marketing team realized that fatigue is easily detected by looking for people yawning.

So they built a scaled-down coffee vending machine — no buttons, nowhere to insert money — with just a single video camera inside powered by facial recognition software that could detect when someone standing in front of it was yawning.

As soon as it detected a yawn, it dispensed a cup of coffee (the cups had the positioning statement BYE BYE RED EYE on them). The machine served more than two hundred cups in a day.

So far, the grocery industry focus-tests things like best location for products, best flow through the store, and so on — using something called concurrent think-aloud (CTA). And yes, it's as irritating as it sounds. CTA is just a fancy way of saying you walk around the store with a researcher, trying to say everything that comes into your head. "I think I'll go right here. Wow, it's really bright here. Where is the aisle sign? There it is. It has smaller letters than I thought it would have."

The problem is, this has never been a very reliable system. For one thing, the researcher is always interfering with the natural process, distracting the subject, and possibly inserting biases. Plus, participants have to think about forming and verbalizing answers to the researcher's questions, which inevitably impacts their decision-making process.

A human business won't need to rely on these kinds of tactics, when they can instead simply observe the subject walk, unimpeded, through the store. This type of study is emerging in a field known as cued retrospective recall (CRR).

Here, the shopper isn't even aware they're being used as a test. Cameras follow their movements around the store, and they're approached as they exit — offered some money for an hour of their time. If they agree, researchers play back their movements in the store and ask them to describe why they did what they did. Subjects don't just get to see where they walked, they get to see exactly where they looked.

Unbeknownst to the shopper, eye-tracking cameras are hidden at the back of a shelf display, recording a heat map of where their eye went.

In CRR results like in this photo, yellow and red mean the subject's eye lingered in those areas longer than in the green areas.

ON THE HORIZON

Matching Ads to Humans

It's one of the big challenges in measuring marketing effectiveness — you spend money on, say, digital-screen advertising in elevators, but you never quite know what type of demographic you're reaching. While the advertising-platform provider can usually provide a general sense of the age and gender of who'll see the ads (more men in Irish pubs, more women in spas, to use an unfortunately gender-stereotyped example), they really don't have a good sense of the audience themselves.

That's changing, and soon the actual displays will be able to measure, in real time, the demographics of people looking at the ad display screen.

One system, set to roll out across Britain, is called OptimEyes. Special video displays have a small video camera in the top, backed by facial-detection software. The software "watches" people who are looking at the monitor at any given second and estimates their gender and age group, in addition to tracking how long they've been looking at the screen. (The company is careful to note that its software is facial-detection, not facial-recognition — it can't identify specific people.)[18]

Across its network, the company can move ads that are targeted at young men, for example, to locations which — at that very moment — seem to have more young men gathering. Or, if a large number of targets are in a few specific locations, the ad's creative itself can be tweaked.

Already, more than six thousand digital advertising displays in public locations are running the system.

Matching Offers to Human Emotions

Taking facial detection one step further is Russia-based marketing tech company Synqera. Its system, called Simplate, detects emotions in shoppers to offer timely promotions based on shoppers' real-time feelings.

It uses touch screen tablets placed at retail checkouts. When shoppers stand near the tablet to pay, software scans their facial expression to determine the emotion they're likely feeling and offers coupons and discounts tied to that feeling. Feeling low? Perhaps this deal might make you feel better! Feeling angry? Perhaps our customer service team can intervene right now for you! Feeling elated? Here's a coupon for next time to brighten your day even more! These offers aim to target shoppers right when a small boost might help them feel more kinship with the brand.

A side benefit is that the aggregated data of shoppers' moods can act as a kind of informal focus group, helping retail brands understand what time of day tends to be most stressful for people, what day of the week people seem happiest, and so on.

Following You Around the Store

File this under *C* for creepy.

Digital agency CUBOCC has worked with Hellmann's (the mayonnaise company) in São Paulo to have smart shopping carts market products on their own.

Shoppers placed a wireless tablet fitted with NFC (near field communication) technology in their cart, and as they walked by certain parts of the supermarket, the tablet would prompt them with recipe suggestions.

As consumers shopped in the produce section, for instance, the tablet detected their proximity to nearby fruits and vegetables and played a video of a summer salad with — of course — Hellmann's mayonnaise in the dressing. If they liked the recipe, they could share it with their friends on social media.

Laugh if you want. Sales rose nearly 70 percent among the forty-five thousand customers who used the system for just one month.

TOUCHPOINTS: FIVE MARKETING TAKEAWAYS

 Technology shines when people find unexpected ways to use it and new ways to bring together old and state-of-the-art, clunky and slick. Technology offers new opportunities to be creative. Find them and run with it.

 It used to be that the best marketing promoted tools. Now the best marketing promotes potential and associates the tool or the manufacturer of the tool with that potential. People want to know they can build a house, not that they should buy a hammer.

 Groundbreaking innovations spawn whole new market categories. This means if you're not constantly challenging yourself and your customers, you're likely to get left behind. Take risks. Do the things no one else is doing.

 Sometimes the greatest clarity can be achieved by saying very little and leaving the audience to complete your ideas in their mind. Saying too much can diminish or even demolish the connection you're making.

 When you can strike an emotional chord with your audience, you win. People will talk about your product and your brand. They'll want to be seen as being connected with you and your values. No technology in the world can replace the biochemical reaction of feeling connected and inspired. Only the people and stories associated with that technology can do that.

CHAPTER 8
WEB/SOCIAL

So we poured our budget into a Foursquare strategy, which we abandoned to pursue an Instagram strategy, which we dropped to pursue a Pinterest strategy. I'm starting to think what we really need is a strategy strategy.

WEB FAIL

A critical component of your communications is how you present yourself online. There's no limit to the number of ways in which organizations make their websites very non-human. Tod's favourite example is the website of an internship program, subsidized by the federal government, that he was investigating for his firm, engageQ digital. The program allows employers to help students get a head start in the emerging media space by covering 75 percent of the students' wages.

But, as usual with far too many large-organization websites, the layers of redundant clicks and processes was mind-boggling.

Check out what happens when an employer tries to apply for the program.

Step One

- Click the "Application Form" link.

- Choose between downloading a PDF form, a second PDF that's a "guide" to the form, and seeing an HTML page with locations of where to send the form.

Okay, first ... PDF forms?! Still?! You know, web pages can handle forms on their own. And how about putting all that info in a single document?

Step Two

- Click the "Form" link.

- Land on a page with a single link on it: "Request this document."

- Click the intermediate link, only to learn that there's no way to download the form — you have to give the government your email address.

Having to click the link twice is as if you clicked a search-result link in Google, and Google then displayed an intermediate page with a single link on it that said "Go to this site." Um, thanks.

But the next step is where it gets absolutely stupid.

Step Three

- Receive this email from the feds: "Confirmation of receipt. Thank you for submitting a document request. We would like to confirm that we have received your request. The document you have requested will be sent in a separate message to this e-mail address shortly."

- Receive, literally one second later, the application form in a separate email.

Sadly, this kind of insanity isn't limited to government websites (though it does seem to be an epidemic there). Far too many organizations have unnecessarily complicated websites that serve only to confuse customers.

In this chapter, we'll explore a more human approach to developing your website and social channels.

CHECKLIST: BUILDING CONNECTIONS/ COMMUNITY

One of the cornerstones of relationship building is the time and attention afforded to connecting with other individuals. This is true of developing personal and professional relationships. In fact, many people will tell you that the foundation of a marriage is communication — actually taking the time to connect and maintain a strong connection with your spouse/partner.

Online community building is no different. It takes time and energy to attract attention and encourage participation. As we often say, it's the aggregate of a million small things rather than a reliance on one big whammy to turn a lot of heads at once (likely at a significant cost) that has the greatest chance of success. Besides, building a community on individual relationships is more manageable because you'll be aware of the individuals and they'll be aware of you. Consider what it's like when you meet and have a chance to speak to a few people directly at a small gathering versus meeting tens or hundreds of people in a few hours at a well-attended lecture, conference, or large social gathering. Who are you more likely to remember? From which event are you more likely to come home with a bundle of disembodied business cards?

Here's a checklist for building connections/community:

- Don't make a big announcement that you've joined a social networking or social media site, or share how you plan to use it to build a large and influential community. Get to know how to use the tool and establish a rhythm and voice before letting people know you're there.

- Make sure you know about the person you are reaching out to or who has initiated a connection with you before making the link. Read that person's profile, review some of their online content, and check out the names and profiles of others with whom they are connected. Make sure there's a common interest or a spark with which to build a relationship.

- Limit yourself to a specific and manageable number of new connections on a daily basis. Don't just make superficial links. Establish the connection through a personalized message. Show them it's a real person, not a robot, at the other end of the connection.

- Provide value for your community, even before you start to build it. Without something meaningful or interesting to act as the central gravity of the community, few people will take the time to skim through or participate. Besides, no one likes showing up to a party when the hosts are just setting up.

- Make it part of your routine to check in with one to five random individuals each day. Let them know you're still there and engaged.

VALUE-BASED COMMUNITIES

The movie *Field of Dreams* gave us the famous quote "if you build it, they will come." It's a great line for a movie. Sadly, we've heard too many people use it to justify their plans to build an online community. Certainly, if you don't build it, no one will come. On the other hand, the mere existence of a gathering place is not enough to result in anything worthwhile.

Building the community is only the construction part of the process, like pouring the foundation and framing a house. Establishing an engaged community — and an engaged community is really what you want — is more of a creative process. In the online world, the real work begins after you cut the ribbon.

Most of the successful web/social communities began not because of a single large-scale contribution, but because of a lot of small ones — just as with building personal relationships. Grand gestures like presenting a cool gathering place is simply part of the process. Remember, to be successful, a restaurant needs to be accessible, have an appealing atmosphere, offer good food and good service, and have prices people are willing to pay. Of course, it helps if one of the elements stands out above the others. Still, service needs to be up there. Most people won't suffer terrible service for a superb gastronomic experience if they can get both (or an average of the two) somewhere else.

And so it goes with online communities. You need to have most of the elements covered yet still offer something to your audience they can't get anywhere else. The business world calls this the "value proposition." Whether your community is intended to support your business, hobby, or political aspirations, you must offer something people can't get anywhere else if you intend to get noticed.

Digital pioneers had the edge. There was little (if any) competition when they launched their communities. In those cases, the value proposition was obvious — they were one of the only (or only) online destinations catering to a given interest. As these communities made the interest more popular, competing online communities (that is to say, new communities serving the same niche) needed to offer a slightly different take in order to be attractive to others.

Here are two examples from Mark's experience.

- The Canadian Podcast Buffet was created by Bob Goyetche and Mark as the first community specifically to promote and support Canadian podcasters and their shows. It had a built-in audience of podcast creators and, as Mark and Bob learned when they loosened the format and had some fun by incorporating interviews and guest hosts, a podcast-listening public. Over time, their audience grew well beyond Canada even though the show was Canadian-centric.

- Just One More Book (JOMB) joined the online effort to promote great children's books and the people who create them, in July 2006. There were already many successful blogs and active communities dedicated to the subject. None were podcasting. So, Mark and Andrea offered something no one else did at the time —the ability to eavesdrop on two people passionately and energetically talking about the books they loved and why they loved them. Listeners could tune in on their computers or portable MP3 players. This led to weekly audio interviews with authors and illustrators —something no one else was doing at the time. Eventually they produced a few videos and a special video series called *Rock Stars of Reading* (again, a fresh idea). Some people say JOMB arrived late and became a standout because it offered something different. Mark and Andrea believe JOMB arrived differently and carved out its own space.

What's important to note about these two examples is the role of interaction, specific and implied. In both cases, there was a rapport between the two hosts which energized the listener. The tone was such that listeners felt present. This was particularly true of JOMB, which was recorded in a coffee shop. Mark and Andrea often received feedback that listeners would wake up ahead of their families, brew some coffee, download the latest episode, then sit in their kitchen or living room, coffee in hand, earbud in ear, and join the hosts, virtually, in the coffee shop.

The atmosphere of the two shows helped build community. Listeners felt connected with the hosts. Both shows enjoyed routine contributions from listeners who felt comfortable reaching out and extending the conversation beyond the regularly released audio files.

Consider our restaurant analogy from earlier: A great restaurant is a destination, has a welcoming atmosphere, quality food, remarkable service, and charges prices people are willing to pay. Your online community requires similar elements.

- **Destination:** Your community must be located in a good and memorable online space. It must also be visually appealing and have a great name and easy-to-remember URL. More importantly, the site should appear welcoming, be easy to navigate, and offer visitors the ability to interact or participate.

- **Atmosphere:** While a slick design which punches out content and avoids clutter is important, atmosphere is more about the tone and activity in the space. This is set in large part by the host of the community, making it very important for the host to immerse him- or herself as an active and committed participant. The host must be a personality rather than a robot. If the host can't be a player or influencer in their own community, it will be nearly impossible to manage a crisis when one emerges.

- **Content:** Valuable, interesting, and entertaining content will help build a dialogue and motivate return visits. Of course, the goal of most communities is to have such an engaged membership that the content creation and sharing parts will take care of themselves. However, the host must be an active participant in the generation and sharing of content — even maintaining a theme or content calendar for at least some days of each week. Hosts who go dark might end up sending a message that their community isn't worth their time — a message with the potential to cascade.

- **Service:** Just as some restaurants have greeters and hosts who make sure you feel important when you arrive, that you're seated quickly and comfortably, and that a server is assigned to take care of you, so, too, should an online community host be concerned about the comfort of their participants. This becomes increasingly difficult if the rate of growth or the size of the community becomes overwhelming. A host can make sure information can be found and that they or prominent members of the community are available to help integrate new members and support the community on an ongoing basis.

- **Tiered access:** Marketers, communicators, and campaign managers love this, hobby folks not so much since conventional thought is that it involves the exchange of money. It doesn't have to. Nor are you obliged to offer tiered access. The principle behind tiered access is giving something else of value for a greater level of participation — be it a click, completed registration form, membership, sponsorship, donation, or purchase.

Relevance extends beyond just the idea of an online community. It must be pervasive throughout the destination, atmosphere, content, service, and value. Perhaps that famous *Field of Dreams* quote needs to be adapted for the online world: "If you're relevant, they will come."

CMSES ARE NOT YOUR FRIEND

Let's get into the specifics now.

Content management systems (CMSes) like Wordpress, Drupal, or Joomla provide a simplified way of publishing content about your organization to the Web and social channels. But these systems are usually not configured to help your employees create content which resonates with your audience and stakeholders.

CMSes are, by definition, simply databases with tables and fields. While most of these tools provide for basic input fields like *Title* (headline) and *Body Text*, they're hardly the best for most companies' needs.

The fields prompt for the most basic information without reminding writers to use human language, to write with the reader in mind, and to keep to corporate communications standards.

To be sure, it's possible to hire a programmer to customize these systems somewhat, but this customization isn't cheap and often requires significant changes to the core code of the CMS, risking its stability.

Luckily, other tools are coming onto the scene to help you publish content to your company's website and maintain a human tone.

One of our favourites is GatherContent. This tool lets you set up content templates which prompt your people to keep tone in mind, re-arrange page elements with more flexibility than Wordpress and similar systems, and make certain fields mandatory.

* Product name

Include the product ID number in brackets after the product name. E.g. "300 watt Hi-fi system (31909)". The ID will be a small grey link to the main product inventory catalogue.

Price (leave this empty if you don't know, financial will review)

GatherContent also has robust team tools which other CMS systems lack, like being able to assign content tasks to specific people or teams, set due dates, discuss content, and flag a page pending review.

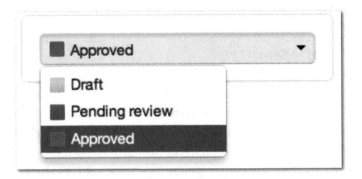

Additionally, one of the tools will let you export approved posts to your Wordpress- or Drupal-based site.

Whichever CMS you opt for, you should ensure it lets you customize the content fields to provide reminders to your team to humanize the content.

Web Forms the Human Way

While we're on the topic of human web workflow, a word about web forms is in order.

Web-based forms like Contact Us pages have replicated the design of paper forms — a flat list of fields followed by a button labelled Submit. (Many forms also have a Clear button, which often leads to people accidentally clearing out their entry — more frustration for your users.)

This structure was informed by database engineers who simply dumped a table structure onto a web page.

A more human approach is to turn the form into something that more closely resembles how people talk.

Here's a great example of human web user-interface (UI) in use by Sharewave. It's a basic Contact Us form but is much friendlier.

Dear Sharewave,

My name is _____ and my email is _____ .

My company name is _____ , and you can find us online at

http:// _____

Please let me know when Sharewave is ready.

Request an Invite

Customizing for Humans

So how do you make your website more human? One smart method is to provide a small amount of customization to hit the right people with what they specifically need.

Here's an example.

Tod's company uses Basecamp — a widely used and respected project management tool. Before Basecamp switched to a new pricing model, its pricing page recommended their ninety-nine-dollar package — the "sweet spot," as the program's makers say.

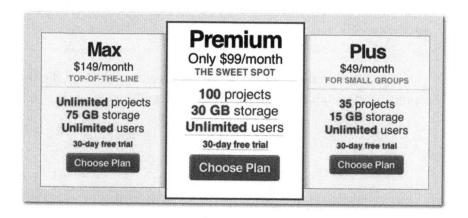

Except, here's the thing: How do Basecamp's makers know what the sweet spot for Tod's company's specific needs are? They don't. They present this plan to everyone. It's a static page.

In fact, the sweet spot for Tod's team happens to be the Plus option, not the one the site highlights.

With even a simple form backed by some programming intelligence, you can provide a more human approach to getting people closer to taking action.

One example of a company that's done a great job is Are My Sites Up?, a white-labelled service for web service agencies to alert their clients when their websites go down. When you click "Pricing," you get this message:

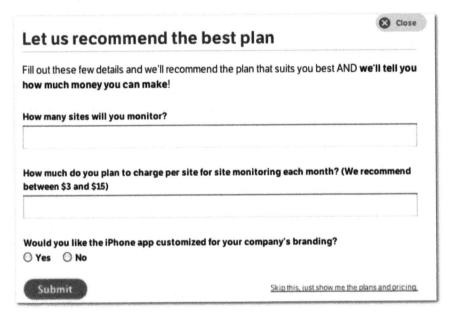

Tod punched in the information for his specific needs, and the site recommended a simpler solution than its default offering.

Of the company's four primary plans, they recommended the low-end one — for Tod's firm's specific needs. Brilliant! And best of all, this type of form isn't a difficult bit of code to program.

Even better, the site calculated that based on the information Tod had entered, he'd lose money and should consider charging his clients more:

> Given your 4 sites and the $5 that you'd like to charge for site monitoring, your recommended plan is: One Custom. You'd make $20 per month, and we'd charge you $40 per month.

THE SWARM METHODOLOGY

Tod was one of the Internet's first podcasters.

In his podcasts, he interviewed regular people about the extraordinary skills they had. He interviewed a pilot about how to start a passenger jet, he talked to Canadian public-radio icon Michael Enright about how to interview, and his esthetician friend, Laura, demonstrated how to wax your hair off — using his ass as the platform (*http://bit.ly/waxmyass*).

But it was a podcast in which he described how to get yourself upgraded on a major airline carrier (even if you didn't have the certificates) that generated the most amount of heat. And, to be fair, the process was a bit deceptive, requiring the truth to be bent a little (read: a lot). He posted the podcast on his site and for a couple of weeks, nothing happened. He got a few comments, but nothing serious.

And then all hell broke loose.

Within hours, Tod's podcast site was overtaken by angry comments saying he was horribly unethical for posting such a show. Worse, comments were associating his relationship with Canada's public broadcaster — the CBC — for whom Tod was a freelance technology columnist, with the podcast. A sample comment:

> Great. Now someone at the CBC is telling us how to lie and steal. This stuff is BS and I am very disappointed

that my tax dollars are going to someone like this to report this garbage. I hope this guy gets yanked off the flight.

Of course, Tod's podcast had nothing to do with his work as a technology columnist at the CBC, but this podcast was beginning to generate heat — within a few hours he had dozens of similar messages saying what a jerk he was for teaching people how to get upgraded for free.

In short, an angry swarm massed around him and it was looking for blood.

As with much of public relations, perception is reality, and he had to move fast to quiet down this angry storm.

The way in which he responded to the feedback became a five-point methodology he uses with clients today — SWARM.

S — Speak with a Human Voice
W — Win/Win
A — Avoid a Public Battle
R — Right the Wrongs
M — Make Friends

We'll get into each of these points in a moment, but for now, here is the response Tod posted:

Hi everyone,

First, thanks for the lively discussion on here! That piece was always intended as a way to generate interest in my hobby podcast, so I'm glad you found it. I am, of course, a bit embarrassed that even as a futurist, I didn't forsee how quickly it would spread.

In reading through your comments, I agree with many of them, so I have pulled that piece from my site. I should have thought more carefully about it.

I did want to clarify a few items:

1. The "How to Do Stuff" podcast is not a CBC production. It is only my own hobby podcast. In fact, I am on sabbatical from the CBC for a couple of years (though I still produce a technology column for them). This has nothing to do with the CBC.

2. CBC staffers do not fly in full-Y class. Policy dictates that they take the lowest possible fare. The only rule exception they have that I'm aware of is that engineers and technicians are permitted to check more than the usual limit of baggage provided the baggage is required broadcast equipment.

3. When I was with CBC, I rarely travelled on their dime. I do tons of flying as a professional speaker (my "day job"). (*http://todmaffin.com/speaking/*)

4. I wasn't aware there was a link to my hobby podcast from the CBC site. I know they are in the process of redesigning that page, and I will ensure that link is removed when the new page launches. Thanks for letting me know.

Anyway, either way, I appreciate your feedback and agree with you that it was probably a podcast I should have kept in my over-caffeinated head.

Tod

PS This looks like a great board and I'm looking forward to participating once this well-deserved lashing is over. ;-)

As soon as he posted this response, the negative feedback stopped in its tracks. Literally. He didn't receive a single negative comment after this post. In fact, only four comments were added after this and they were all positive.

And it was all because he managed the swarm. Here's how you can too when — not if — it happens to you.

SWARM — *S*: Speak with a Human Voice

Organizations have a bad habit of communicating with people as if they were, well, organizations. They speak in grand tones of "we" and "us" — trying very hard to avoid admitting that an actual human being ("I" and "me") wrote the text. Words like "we" and "us" serve only to distance yourself from your correspondent and, in a crisis situation, this is the last thing you want to do. Rather, you want people to identify with you and feel like you're both in it together.

Speaking like a human is all about tone. Remember, these are *social* networks — so your tone should be social in nature.

Tod's response to the podcast-haters was deliberately written using the same manner of speech as he uses verbally. Informal, pleasant, and grateful for the feedback.

Imagine your Twitter monitoring tool (you *do* have one, right?) picks up someone who tweets this:

> What horrible service I just got at Fake Tires, Inc. Mechanic totally tried to screw me over and bill me three times what that battery costs!

Before social networks, if your company got this in the form of a mailed letter, you might have responded in an organizational voice:

> We're sorry to hear of the issues you're having. Thank you for letting us know.

It sounds trite and one almost expects to see a file name at the bottom, C:\Templates\GoAway.doc, giving away the fact that someone at your firm just copied and pasted from a form letter. Classy.

Instead, you should speak with your own, human voice. Display the emotions that a normal human would.

If you didn't, in fact, work for Fake Tires, Inc., and this person was a friend of yours telling you this story, you certainly wouldn't say: "Gee, David, this is something which is very unfortunate. I trust that the matter will be resolved in an expeditious manner. Thank you for telling me the details of your experience."

No, you'd probably express some degree of surprise, empathy, and concern for your friend's feelings. Just because you work for Fake Tires, Inc., doesn't mean you shouldn't respond like you would if you were face to face with someone.

A good Twitter response might be:

"Yikes — I'm so sorry to hear this happened. That certainly isn't the kind of service we strive for. Pls DM [direct message] me. I'll follow up directly. ^Tod"

Even though this is under 140 characters (the maximum message length on Twitter), there's a lot going on here. Let's break this response down.

- **"Yikes."** There's no "yikes" in the corporate dictionary, and that's precisely why you should use it, or something like it. Think honestly about what your natural reaction was to that tweet. What did your inner voice say? It probably said "Yikes" or "Oh no" or "Egads." Those are the very words you should use. It shows that you're a real person with real feelings too. In our experience, an honest starter word like this has been able to de-escalate an issue by itself.

- **"I'm so sorry to hear this happened."** It's okay to apologize. In our own work on client accounts, we sometimes make a point to add the word "so" in that sentence. Somehow, it adds an extra layer of honesty. Again, an organization might say "We're sorry," but only a human would say "I'm so sorry." As well, there is a pervasive myth in the corporate world that suggests that if you apologize you are now somehow legally liable. It's not true. You can feel sorry that someone had a bad experience. That doesn't mean you have to comp them their entire car-repair bill.

- **"That certainly isn't the service we strive for."** Remember that in a public tweet conversation, it's not just you and the person who's angry who are seeing these messages — anyone who follows both your account and the angry person's account will see this. An example: In addition to a bunch of friends, Tod follows his local cable company's tech support Twitter account (@shawhelp). At least once or twice a month, he'll see in his Twitter stream that a friend is having problems with their account or service. How Shaw treats his friend is important to him and may change his opinion of them when it comes time to renew his service.

- **"Please DM me."** In Twitterspeak, this means to send a (private) direct message. As we'll discuss later, you will want to take this discussion off-line as fast as you can. Acknowledge the message, thank the person, apologize if necessary, and move the discussion behind closed virtual doors. This will then keep the discussion off the Twitter stream of those who follow both you and your correspondent.

- **"I'll follow up directly."** This might be the most important part of the message — you, personally, are making a direct commitment. This is a much stronger statement than "We will follow up," which, frankly, nobody believes. Think about it: If you got a letter back from a company saying "We will look into the matter," do you really expect they will? Probably not. But again, by using first-person pronouns ("I," in this case), you reinforce the fact that there's a human being behind your tweet and that you yourself will look into it.

- **"^Tod."** This caret symbol (^) is a Twitter convention that identifies the person typing. If you work for a large organization, you might be using this. In most cases we've seen, the convention has been to use initials, like ^TM. We strongly recommend you use a real first name instead since it's easier for people to identify with a name than a set of initials. This also reinforces the commitment you made earlier. Some organizations set up a Twitter account for each individual person — like Canadian mobile-phone provider Fido. In such a case, using the caret convention is unnecessary.

In addition to Speaking Like a Human, there is actually a second important *S* as well — and that's to Size Up the commenter. By checking a user's Klout score or finding out how many Facebook friends they have, you'll have a rudimentary sense of the impact their words. Someone with a Klout score (Klout is a measure of Internet influence) of sixty-five or higher could create enough buzz to cause additional damage, as their original post gets amplified by their followers. This isn't to suggest you should only respond to high-impact people — far from it — but if you have a number of comments to respond to within limited time, a simple triage like determining their rough influence level might help you prioritize your responses.

SWARM — *W*: Win/Win

"Stand up!" boomed the leader at the conference Tod was attending. "And find a partner."

He cringed. Honestly, as a participant, Tod prefers *zero* interaction with others in the room. He'd much rather just absorb information from the speaker than participate in any ice-breaking exercises. It's not that he's anti-social; he just learns best on his own. Perhaps it's his only-child tendencies coming out.

But everyone stood up. An over-caffeinated woman in her twenties bounced up to him. "Hey — you can be my partner! We'll win this thing, whatever it is."

The session leader explained the rules. "Hold your palms up against each other." Tod's partner jabbed her hands at him. He reciprocated. "Now then. I'm going to start a timer for twenty seconds. Whoever can get their partner to move their feet, wins." His timer beeped, and Tod's perky partner began pushing at his hands, trying to throw him off balance. He tried the same, in some kind of bizarre corporate-approved arm wrestle. Neither of them moved their feet and the timer went off.

"Stop! So, how many of you employed the brute-force method of just pushing as hard as you could?" A few hands were raised. "How many of you relaxed your arms, so your partner would fall into you, causing their feet to move?" A few snickers, and more hands.

"And how many of you BOTH won?"

Confused silence filled the room. "Did any of you agree to BOTH move your feet so you would both win?"

A fellow in the back yelled out, "You said the first person who moved their feet lost."

"No I didn't. I said 'Whoever can get their partner to move their feet, wins.' There's no reason why you both couldn't have won if you'd just agreed to both move your feet."

Sometimes we forget that just because one person wins doesn't mean the other person has to lose. With just a little bit of thought, it's not difficult to construct a scenario where both people win.

People will complain on your social media channels because they want something to change — better service on their next visit, a cheaper rate, and so on. One way to help knock down an angry swarm is to give them something more than just a response.

Give them a win.

In the case of his airline-upgrade podcast response, Tod removed the podcast episode in question and told his listeners so. "I have pulled that piece from my site. I should have thought more carefully about it." Honestly, the episode wasn't all that important to him, and taking it down gave them the satisfaction of knowing they had made some change.

You don't need to overthink this. Wins can be simple — a promise to check back with someone to see if something they were complaining about has improved.

Tod's company works with a number of shopping centres to help them manage their social media channels. One day, a Facebook page they moderate for one of these centres started to blow up. A visitor had posted a complaint about the in-mall kiosk vendors. These vendors sell everything from cellphone covers to makeup to inexpensive jewellery. Apparently, some of the vendors could be quite aggressive in their sales approach — even going so far as grabbing passers-by by their arm to try to pull them over to their kiosks.

The visitor complained about the aggressive kiosk people and her comment got an enormous amount of traffic — dozens of comments and likes a minute after her opening salvo was posted.

Tod's approach to responding was twofold: One, acknowledge the comments and promise to look into the problem; and, two, report back to the community the next morning on what happened.

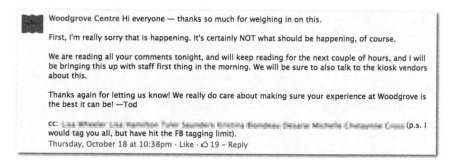

Every dozen or so comments, Tod — posting as the shopping centre's brand — would dive into the comments with something like this:

Woodgrove Centre Hi ~~Julia Demki, Liz Ranger, Janis Jonsson, Annabud Seula , Vi Mfumfu, Daphne Peter~~ — thanks for letting us know! See our response above. We'll check into this first thing in the morning. —Tod

Woodgrove Centre ~~you Assent Annette Dema Tina Linden Beneby of Jame Christine Row Hedi Lette Farley~~
Thanks so much for taking a moment tonight to tell us about this. We'll take this up with the kiosk people first thing in the morning and make sure they understand this isn't acceptable. I'm sorry that you had that experience, and we will do what we can to fix it. 😊 Have a great night! —Tod

Woodgrove Centre ~~Amy Au Deanna Nelson Kelly Laguna Myra I amosse an RaCome Karen Verna Nadine Edwards~~ Thank you so much — I have already placed this on the agenda for mall management to discuss as soon as possible (probably first thing in the morning), and we'll make sure we speak with the kiosk people to ensure you don't have this experience again. I'm very grateful you took a second tonight to let us know, and please don't hesitate to Message me through this page if you have any other comments! —Tod 😊

Woodgrove Centre ~~LaRuke Mach Corinne Park Denture Sharon Ferguson~~ — thank you so much for letting us know about this! We'll be addressing this in the morning at both the mall management level AND with the kiosk people. This obviously is not the experience we want guests to have, so I'll make sure we put steps in place to have them tone it down. 😊 —Tod

He tagged the major combatants so that they'd be notified when a response had been posted. Then he waited for another dozen comments to come in and post essentially the same thing, worded differently.

As soon as he started with this approach, comments died down almost instantly. People felt they were being listened to, which is half the reason they posted in the first place: to be heard. Tod's responses impressed them even more because this was taking place in the evening, outside of business hours.

The next morning, mall management spoke to the kiosk vendors, gave them another copy of the selling guidelines, and threatened them with fines if more reports of aggressive tactics were reported. Of course, Tod reported this in the comment stream, to keep people updated:

Woodgrove Centre Hi everyone. I wanted to give you an update on where we stand with the retailers who were overly earnest in their approach.

Ten days ago (Oct 9), our Specialty Leasing Manger (she oversees the relationships with our temporary retailers) gave each retailer another copy of Woodgrove's Solicitation Guidelines, which include very clear instructions against aggressive sales techniques. We monitor their compliance closely and just this morning sent them all an email reminding them of this commitment as well as personally speaking to them when they opened.

We will also begin random checking from herein to make sure your experience at Woodgrove is the best it can be.

I'll be reaching out to some of you personally as well to ask if you'd be willing to let us contact you in a few months to let us know if it has gotten better.

Thank you again so much for letting us know your concerns. We know you have lots of shopping options on the Island and we really value that you choose to spend some of your time with us!

Please don't hesitate to click the Message button on our Page if you'd like to follow up. —Tod
Friday, October 19 at 11:05am · Like · 👍 9 - Reply

So the win there was that the comments actually resulted in something real happening. Then, Tod sent a message to about fifty of the most active commenters.

Facebook, unfortunately, lumps all messages from brand pages into a generic Other Messages bucket which most people don't check, so only about fifteen people got back to him. Each one was happy to be contacted later. Tod filed their email addresses away and reached out to them a couple of months later to see if things had gotten any better.

Finding the right win is critical to dealing successfully with a negative response.

Done right, when they win, you win.

SWARM – *A*: Avoid a Public Battle

Perhaps the biggest mistake we see organizations make online is getting ensnared in a debate about an issue on a public channel — whether that's a blog, Facebook page, Twitter account, or somewhere else.

Once you identify an issue and reach out to the combatant (for lack of a better term), you should take the issue off-line.

There are many ways to do this, but the simplest is to ask the person to email you the details.

- If the issue shows up on Twitter, ask them to follow your brand account so you can DM them your direct email address, then continue the conversation that way.

- If the issue shows up on Facebook, ask them to send you a private message to your brand page, then continue the conversation there.

- If the issue shows up on your blog, ask them to send you an email to your corporate account, then continue the conversation there.

- Remember, during an attack (even one which is only a simple complaint) you have TWO audiences — the person who raised the issue and everyone else who's reading. Express concern, tell everyone you're going to work on the issue, and move the combatant off-line.

NEVER HAVE A PUBLIC FIGHT IN FULL VIEW OF THE REST OF THE SWARM.

Have you ever had an email or Twitter fight with a friend? The more you go back and forth, the more the usually tiny issue escalates and before you know it, you're not speaking to each other for a year. This is the nature of a tit-for-tat discussion — you will never, ever win.

Acknowledge the issue and move it off-line.

SWARM – *R*: Right the Wrongs

You may find that in the heat of the moment, people exaggerate an issue. Suddenly, a simple dispute over what they were charged becomes, in their mind, a criminal action where they were billed hundreds of thousands of dollars.

One of the peculiarities of this — call it digital personality disorder — is that combatants believe they won't get attention without a very serious story. So, they might add details that simply aren't accurate.

Imagine you got a tweet like this:

I use a wheelchair and tried getting into your restaurant Friday. Your elevator was packed with people who are perfectly capable of taking the stairs. (Plus, it's out of order half the time.) #fail

---

First, try to calm down the instinctive defensive feeling this creates in you. Think — does this person have a real point? Perhaps that elevator really is, in fact, being jammed up by able-bodied people who could easily take the stairs. Always look for a Win/Win. This might be a great one for you.

But almost certainly, your elevator hasn't been broken "half the time," as this person claims.

It's important that you correct the record. Remember, Google has an elephant's memory. If she posted this in a blog review, you need to have the accurate information attached to this post, so correcting the record right on that page as a comment is critical. If she posted this on a consumer review site like Yelp, there's nothing you can do to get her comment removed from your listing.

There is nothing wrong with politely correcting the record, and you should absolutely do it if someone has claimed something that isn't true.

In this case, you might respond something like this:

> Thank you for letting me know about this. I'm so sorry that happened to you last Friday. [S — Speak Like a Human]

> I've instructed our team to put a sign in the elevator asking people to use the stairs if they don't have mobility issues. [W — Win/Win]

> Please let me know directly at manager@restaurant.com if you have any other concerns. [A — Avoid a Public Battle]

> The elevator is almost always working, though. It hasn't been broken half the time. [R — Right the Wrongs]

> Could I pick your brain in the future about ways we can make our restaurant more accessible? [M — Make Friends]

There is nothing wrong with politely correcting inaccuracies. In fact, you should do it. Just do it in a human, polite tone.

SWARM – *M*: Make Friends

The final, and perhaps most important, part of the SWARM methodology is to turn your combatants into advocates.

In the case of the previous section, when a wheelchair-using guest had issues with accessibility in the restaurant, a simple way to make friends is to use her as a kind of informal focus group on access. Always ask permission, though, before this kind of move. Done with tact and a genuine desire to improve, almost nobody will turn you down.

It's simple to do — you don't need special mailing-list software or web-based bulletin boards. Just create a folder in your email program for each issue and store your new friends' emails there.

In the case of a restaurant, your issue-based folders could be:

- Improve access for wheelchairs.

- When are we getting gluten-free bread?

- Patio is too noisy.

- Website is too hard to order from.

Then, once you've made some real improvement in these areas, send a single email back to these people (but only if they gave you permission to do so when the issue first came up). Remember to speak like a human — me and I, not us and we.

Here's a sample email:

Subject: Can I buy you dinner?

Hi Dave,

Last year, you were kind enough to let me know about the problems you were having trying to order food for delivery from our website. Thank you again for your time describing the issue.

Last week, we launched a new version of the website and tried to incorporate many of your great suggestions.

I would love it if you would try ordering again, and please use the coupon code DINNERFORDAVE. That one-time coupon will cover the cost of food up to $50.

If you have any other suggestions or comments on the new site, please send them directly my way. I really appreciate your input!

("Sign" your real name and title.)

The other advantage to making friends in social channels is that this kind of direct service engenders more than fans — it can create advocates for your brand as well. If you're attacked online, these people often will rally to your side.

For this reason, you may want to use Twitter's "lists" function or Google+'s "circles" function to keep a list of your best supporters, categorized by specific topic. Just be sure, if you use a Twitter list, that you set it to private so others can't see the people on that list.

(Facebook doesn't have an easy way for brand pages to delineate their fans into different groups.)

CASE STUDY: APPLEBEE'S

Whenever there's a social media crisis, it's always amusing to watch the armchair quarterbacks crawl out of the woodwork to cast their opinion on what the company should have done better.

Such was the case when an Applebee's server felt stiffed because they didn't get a tip from an ordained pastor who was dining at the restaurant. Instead of a tip, the pastor had written "I give God 10% why do you get 18?" on the line where the gratuity should have gone.

The server's colleague grabbed the receipt, took a photo of it, and posted it to the popular website Reddit, with the headline "My mistake sir, I'm sure Jesus will pay for my rent and groceries."

Posting the photo, however innocuously meant, was a violation of Applebee's policy of protecting its customers' privacy. The server who posted the photo was fired.

Queue the Internet outrage.

Thousands of comments began piling up on the company's various social media channels, like:

> That pastor shouldn't be able to get away with her actions. I can't believe you would allow a customer to bully you after she mistreated one of your hard working servers. Good thing we stopped eating there ages ago so no need to boycott.

> You REALLY messed up Applebee's. I'd like you to know I'm never going to your restaraunt [*sic*] again and will share this story with everyone I know. You dun goofed.

> I will not eat at Applebees ever again.

How the company responded became fodder for these armchair quarterbacks, many of whom railed against Applebee's for "mismanaging" the crisis.

Really? Let's analyze exactly what Applebee's did.

1. **A Thoughtful and swift public response:** First, the company posted a single statement on its Facebook page. It used simple language, expressed genuine regret (but fell somewhat short of an apology), and closed the book on the issue.

> We wish this situation hadn't happened. Our Guests' personal information — including their meal check — is private, and neither Applebee's nor its franchisees have a right to share this information publicly. We value our Guests' trust above all else. Our franchisee has apologized to the Guest and has taken disciplinary action with the Team Member for violating their Guest's right to privacy.

2. **In-stream responses:** Then — and this is what earned the ire of the quarterbacks — the company began responding to individual people directly in the comment stream of the Applebee's Facebook page posts.

About Anonymous Comments

Of course, you don't just need to boost the human factor in your own web/social spaces; you should strive to create a safe and human space for your fans, customers, and prospects.

Newspapers have historically managed the public feedback system through letters to the editor, a feature that allows members of the public to attach their opinions to their names and general locations. Generally, most media prints a full range of opinions — from support of the stories and their characters to opinion that takes an opposing view.

Since adding online commenting to their digital editions, news services have opened a platform for anonymous commenting — in many ways welcoming the wild frontier of opinion. The result is the sharing of many ill- or misinformed opinions, vitriol, and ad hominem attacks.

For example ...

- In the comments on *Ottawa Citizen* columnist Jamie Portman's piece about the screening of the film *Iranium* and heritage minister James Moore's intervention to ensure the screening went ahead as scheduled, "Paddy19" wrote: "What a total BS article. Moore is right and you are wrong. Quit making excuses for people who shut down free speech or hopefully the next person silenced is you. Keep voting Liberal, you loser."

- In response to a *CBC.ca* story about an Ottawa Police special constable who was pricked by a needle of an HIV- and hepatitis-positive detainee, thus facing an uncertain future and a possible horrible death, "Socialistboy" wrote: "Deal with it or get another job…. Suck it up Buttercup!"

- And "pindybindy" commented on a *Globe and Mail* article about Jack Layton and the Senate: "Are you still around Jack? Are you and your wife still double dipping, each getting expenses for one place? Huh?"

These comments bring about many questions. Are Paddy19, Socialistboy, pindybindy, and the countless other people who hide behind anonymity so ashamed of their opinions that they don't want to put their names to them? Are the media organizations unwilling to enforce a real-name-and-location policy for commenters?

Another illustrative example involves an opinion piece by Mark's former Fleishman-Hillard colleague, Honourable Monte Solberg. In his essay "Web comments sections drip with poison," Monte suggests that web-based anonymity encourages people to leave baseless, hateful comments on news articles. As if to prove Solberg's thesis, a commenter who went by the handle *old-timer* left a wordy tirade that dripped with poison. That comment has since been removed.

Mark took the matter to Twitter — "How come newspapers only print signed letters yet allow anonymous web comments?" — and received the following among the replies:

@eel_trebor (Rob Lee of Guelph, Ontario):
I suspect 2 reasons: newsroom trad'n = letters need a verifiable source; reality of net = anon comments drive traffic = ad $$$

@tgrevatt (Treena Grevatt of Ottawa, Ontario):
I think anonymous commenting should go, comment quality in Can media is appalling.

@bsdeluxe (Bob Sherron of St. Louis, Missouri):
Because 99% of papers don't "get" the web.

@suzemuse (Sue Murphy of Ottawa, Ontario):
because newspapers *still* don't get how social media works.

@bobledrew (Bob Ledrew of Ottawa, Ontario):
anon comments remind us all that evolution is a two-way process.

@melimel37 (Melissa Margles of Montreal, Quebec):
b/c the anon comments r the ones where people unleash their inner thoughts that they would NEVER sign their name to!

Ottawa Citizen columnist Kate Heartfield jumped in as well. She pointed out that it's much easier to verify the identity of the writers of ten letters to the editor each day than it would be to verify the identify of the many people who sign up for commenting accounts on a daily basis.

Give serious thought to eliminating anonymous commenting on your organization's blog. The simplest way to execute this is to use Facebook's commenting platform on your site. This requires people to use their real names (or, at least, the name they told Facebook was theirs) in their posts.

If your comment is worth sharing, it's worth attaching your name to. Accountability forces people to be thoughtful about how they express themselves — a sort of self-moderation.

MAKING HUMAN CONNECTIONS ONLINE

Sometimes, your organization's social communications will involve start-ing a "cold" conversation. On some networks, like Twitter, this is as easy as tweeting someone. Other channels, like the popular business-to-business network LinkedIn, require you to request a connection to start interacting with another user. There is a right and wrong way to handle this.

How often have you gone to a conference, met someone, exchanged business cards, found the person on LinkedIn, and then clicked on "Send a Connection Request" with the site's default "I'd like to add you to my professional network on LinkedIn" prepared message?

How would you have done this before LinkedIn? Would you have phoned the person to thank them for the conversation? Or maybe you prefer email? Perhaps you'd have invited the person out for coffee, lunch, or a game of golf to deepen the relationship?

What happened to follow-up? Did someone kill it and not send us the memo?

We're now steeped in a culture in which we robotically send invi-tations written by a software designer and mindlessly accept received invitations because not accepting would be rude, thus building a stock-pile of connections with people we don't really know and eventually aren't sure we even met. And this behaviour is facilitated by services like LinkedIn, which provide the default connection request.

Is that the way you run your business? We hope not. Which presents the question, is that the way you should manage your relationships?

Convenience has become the enemy of meaningful connections and gestures to deepen relationships. Imagine if the Friend, Like, and Connect buttons were replaced with Trust buttons. We would almost certainly reduce the number of people associating themselves with one another and with various brands and organizations. It would also likely impact the pitch and value of discussion. A quality-over-quantity paradigm shift, to use to some buzzwordy lingo.

This culture-of-convenience is further entrenched by the fact that it's been embraced by companies, organizations, governments, political operatives, and even your professional and personal contacts. True, it's much easier and takes less time to use form letters. However helpful and expedient this approach may be, and regardless of the fact that we've resigned ourselves to its necessity, these conveniences do little to build the kind of relationship that would have community members "go to the mattress" for the other party in the relationship.

There is some hope, though. Every now and then, you'll receive an invitation which reinforces the meeting and makes an effort to deepen the relationship. These people set the bar higher and amplify how weak the canned invitation really is.

One such invitation was sent to Mark by author Jane Jordan-Meier after the two met at the 2011 International Association for Business Communicators' World Conference in San Diego.

Join my network on LinkedIn
Jane Jordan-Meier
June 14, 2011 6:07 PM

Hi Mark - I enjoyed our chat at the IABC Conference on the "triangular approach" - really just like Canadians too! Do check out my book and let's keep in touch. I'd like to add you to my professional network on LinkedIn.

- Jane Jordan-Meier

Thank you, Jane! Yes. And, Mark accepted.

It's not rocket science. It's relationship-building effort rather than reflexive network-building.

The Difference Between "Network" and "Connect"

Like many others, we've amassed large numbers of online friendships. Many of them were the result of being early adopters who attended many social media events. It became an early practice to "friend" or "connect" with other registered attendees whether or not you had met one another.

Shocked by how many names his Facebook friends comprised and inspired by a friend-network cleaning by his wife, Mark began removing the names of some of the 1,300 people he apparently knew, scaling back to the names he had interacted with, or expected that he would. It was an attempt to bring the size of his network closer to Dunbar's Number.[19]

Mark managed to shrink his network from over 1,300 to about 500 people. That meant unfriending a lot of "friends." We suspect most didn't notice. It's likely some did and were offended.

Four months after his culling exercise, Mark received a note from Larry. The two had co-presented at a conference several years earlier and had maintained a periodic friendship on Facebook. Larry had discovered he was no longer Mark's Facebook friend and was concerned he might have offended Mark with a comment he'd left on one of Mark's Facebook posts.

Larry's comment hadn't hit a nerve. There was clearly no malice in his online posting nor in Mark's unfriending him some months earlier. However, the incident kicked off an interesting exchange which reminds us about the nature of in-person and online relationships.

Many of our online connections with people we've only briefly met or have met only online are more genuine and fulfilling than relationships we have with people with whom we interact in our own neighbourhoods. Some of our online friends from around the world are more likely to roll up their sleeves and help us achieve our goals than people we see several times a week.

The confusion lies in the word "friend." Facebook has reinvented the word to mean something analogous to "a form of online acquaintance." It's also a bit of a legacy feature, in that specifying someone as a friend in the early days of Facebook was the shorthand way of what is now "Subscribe," which allows you to follow someone's updates without being a so-called friend.

We're happy to report that Mark and Larry are Facebook friends again.

ON THE HORIZON

SoLoMo

SoLoMo, a short-form term for social-local-mobile technology, epitomizes how geo-location capabilities for smart phones are reshaping how we use the Web and interact with each other, find places, restaurants, services, and even other people. SoLoMo is a mobile-centric means of adding entries to search engine results in real time. Apps like Tinder demonstrate the enormous potential for this kind of technology.

Loosely described as a dating app, Tinder enables potential meet-ups based on the location of users, who can define their desired distance range depending on their preferences of proximity. The future of social media will continue to harness this real-time geo-location information and shape how social networks work, maximizing relationships and presenting new means for marketers to reach people with their messaging.

Native Content and Emergent Distribution Platforms

It's not surprising that we've seen a drastic change in how we consume entertainment; while television is far from dead, it has had to change its strategy in terms of attracting viewers and maintaining relevance, even adopting built-in social participation strategies, such as viewers voting on a show's outcome via social media and news anchors urging people to use a specific hashtag when discussing a particular topic. Technology and media-content producers have to adapt to a consumer-driven market and listen to their audience's wants and needs versus blindly foisting content on them any which way.

The explosion of web-only series also speaks to this shift in where and how audiences are taking in content; traditional film and TV delivery channels are being forced to evolve or die, so to speak. Business models for digital content distribution are changing drastically, like many other entertainment industry models, with licence- and service-based delivery models replacing more traditional sales-based distribution funnels.

Given the technological advancements of SoLoMo technologies and how they fit into the way media and entertainment are disseminated, the battlefield for content and media domination is somewhat like the Wild West. The dominant model for delivering entertainment-focused content is currently being hard fought by big power players like Netflix, Amazon, Microsoft, Apple, and Google along with the cable companies; the outcome has yet to be determined. Netflix experimented with subscription-based services for original content, of which HBO was the originator, with the series *House of Cards*, and Amazon and Microsoft appear to be following suit.

The Bleeding Edge

It's no surprise that humans are highly sense-motivated creatures; we yawn while watching a passenger across from us on the subway yawn. We see someone experiencing an emotional moment in a film and might tear up along with them. We like eating, we like music, we like massages, we like seeing, tasting, touching, and feeling things. It makes sense that the devices we use and the online spaces we visit are slowly shifting to accommodate our most innate and instinctive behaviours and preferences, and are getting to know us in a more intimate way; so much so that they could eventually start predicting our behaviour. Sound scary? There's more.

We may even have thought-recognition capability by 2030 thanks to an estimated ten-thousand-fold improvement in computing power. This is being dubbed "telepathic technology" and ushers in a futuristic-sounding but very possible era of brain/computer interfaces and devices with emotion recognition capabilities. Computers are becoming more and more intuitive thanks to rapidly accelerating advancements in NBIC (nanotechnology, biotechnology, information technology and cognitive science) technology. They are getting better at understanding how our minds and moods work and are reacting in a more personalized way. Sound like part of the plot in the movie *Her*? Not too far off. *Forbes* contributor Greg Satell points out that "these systems will know us better than our best friends [do] but will also be connected to the entire Web of Things as well as the collective sum of all human knowledge." These advancements could also be paving the way for the end of anonymity, where technology like biometrics, sensors, and drones make it hard for just about anyone to get off the proverbial digital grid.

TOUCHPOINTS: FIVE WEB/SOCIAL MEDIA TAKEAWAYS

 Web technologies and social networks provide online destinations over which we can both connect and hide. The problems people often blame on technology are really social problems that play out on technology. Remember that in your own activities.

 When you invite participation from others, and when you decide to accept invitations to participate, ask yourself what you're hoping to achieve. Sometimes you may not know until you carefully review your prepared message. Ask yourself if what you're about to release will pave the way to a positive or productive outcome.

 Many web conventions can lead to monotony and missed opportunities. Break people's expectations. Make them take notice by design rather than by expectation.

 Being too concise can sometimes impact clarity as we trim words and leave too much to interpretation and take too much for granted. Take the time to make sure your audience understands you. Being misunderstood can have disastrous results, especially if you're already dealing with a crisis.

 Standing out can be achieved by as little as being decisive and by articulating your message as you would in a one-on-one exchange. Look past the glass in front of you and see a person. Surprise people.

CHAPTER 9

HUMAN RESOURCES

Mike, Carmel, you go to the garden store and get five bags of lime. Dana, Gord, Jill, get me a tarp and carpet, then check Google Earth for a secluded stretch of highway. The rest of you, you'll help me bury the facilitator... who, ironically, has apparently just led the most successful team-building exercise in our company's history.

One of the things we've really focused on since hiring employee number one is building a culture by design, rather than by default. The culture is very important to us. We really think this makes us different as a company and we use that as a starting point. We decided we needed to make everything about our online presence show our company's personality. That may not be for everyone and that's okay. We're not trying to please everyone. If we put ourselves out there and show what we're all about then hopefully people will identify that and it will resonate for them. Ultimately, that's what we want — to connect with people in person.

— MARTIN PERELMUTER, PRESIDENT, SPEAKERS' SPOTLIGHT

TRUST YOUR PEOPLE

Trust, but Verify

Jocelyn only wanted to make a quick call to check in with her friends about going out for dinner after work. But, true to company policy, she needed to drop by her manager's office and ask permission first.

"Sorry, explain why again?" her boss asked.

Jocelyn felt embarrassed. "I haven't seen them in a year. It'll only be a quick call, I promise."

Her boss sighed, stood up, and walked Jocelyn over to the employee phone station, a small room that had only a desk and a phone. "Do you have to be in here with me?" Jocelyn asked. "Sorry," her boss said. "Policy."

Of course, this is fiction. Or is it?

Maybe not. Far too many organizations block their employees from accessing the Internet for personal use. The outdated theory goes that employees are generally up to no good and given an inch, they'll take a mile with such basic privileges.

This management practice even has a name: Theory X — first noted by Douglas McGregor at the MIT Sloan School of Management in the 1960s.

In this theory, employees are assumed to basically be lazy cogs who will avoid any kind of work, requiring constant micro-managed oversight from their superiors. This spawns a bloated hierarchy and overwhelming controls. Sadly, Theory X is still in use in many organizations.

It's silly.

Whenever clients tell us they block sites like Facebook from their employees, we nod our heads in faux understanding and ask, "And I trust you've blocked all external calls as well?"

This usually gets a blank stare, a pause, and then, "Uh, no. Why would we do that?"

Why indeed?

Facebook, Twitter, and other social websites form part of our basic communication these days. Blocking your employees from those sites sends only one message: We don't trust you.

After all, Theory X would state, if we let them access Facebook, they'll just spend all their time reading their news feed and gabbing with their friends.

But what's stopping those same employees from spending all day on the phone talking to their friends? Nothing. They don't do it because they have a sense of responsibility.

Besides, when you think about it, abuse of the Internet is far more trackable than abuse of the phone. Countless tools exist that can keep tabs on your employees' use of the Internet — right down to each person, every website, and every second of use.

This isn't to say, of course, that some people won't abuse access by spending an inappropriate amount of time online. With those people, you warn them to not do it again, and if they keep doing it, you fire them. Just as you would if they spent six hours each day on the phone talking to their friends.

As Ronald Reagan once said during the Cold War: "Trust, but verify."

It's not rocket science.

Sadly, it's not just with Internet use that employers are unnecessarily distrustful. If our employees are sick, we make them bring in evidence of a visit to the doctor. If they need to attend a funeral, we make them bring in a funeral notice.

A human organization trusts its people. It creates a culture where people believe in the mission of the organization, so much that they simply don't want to abuse time.

Creating permission for personal calls, for occasionally checking Facebook messages over lunch, or for taking a half-day off work just because they need a break will, paradoxically, foster far more trust in you. It'll be better for the bottom line. And your people will be happier.

Stop Managing the Minority

Part of the problem lies in human resources managers spending their time setting up procedures to follow when people fail, rather than establishing encouraging TOUCHpoints to help people succeed.

Human resources executive Jillian Walker says that many HR departments operate under the assumption that their people will screw up.

"So, they create policies, they create guidelines, and they create rulebooks, in order to manage the very small percentage that are going to be the ones to screw it up. Instead, put a little bit of structure in place to ensure that employees can thrive, while giving flexibility and autonomy to make decisions. This way, they'll feel like they are empowered," says Walker.

"And then, if trouble comes down the line, you manage the trouble on a one-on-one basis rather than punishing everyone else just in case [some employees] fail. The better approach is really educating people on what being a brand ambassador means and the risk of them saying the wrong thing to the community. And really explaining to them that they are the face of the organization."

For Walker, who's managed human resources in both the private and public sectors, humanizing your HR department comes down to simple conversations.

"Lots of it comes down to just being real with someone and saying, 'Here's how we work and do you buy into this?'"

HUMAN HIRING

Finding the right people — those who have that alchemic combination of skills, attitude, and availability — has never been easy.

Businesses still mostly rely on the traditional methods of finding and hiring people — advertise, conduct interviews, then onboard.

This isn't to suggest all three steps don't need to be done. But there are far more human approaches to recruiting that the savvy manager needs to consider. Here are a few you might want to use.

Flash Tweetups

Without any advance publicity, announce on your company's Twitter account that you're doing a "tweetup" for people who might be interested in working for you. (Tweetups are just a time and place for people to gather and meet up, announced on Twitter.) Either crash a coffee shop (if you're expecting a small number of people) or book part or all of a lounge for larger groups.

The agenda should be simple — one person should give a short (no more than ten minutes) informal presentation (no slides or microphones) about what your organization stands for, what it does, and what you offer employees better than anyone else. Then, just mingle and circulate. Answer questions. Make appointments for further follow-up.

Flash Tweetups can provide you two key advantages. First, if you're seeking people who tend to be spontaneous and extroverted by nature, this will provide a healthy pool of that personality type. Second, since a tweetup is held in a less formal environment, people won't be as guarded as they would be in an office setting.

Twapplications

For jobs in the tech field or in communications departments, understanding the mechanics of social media channels like Twitter is a non-negotiable skill. One marketing agency in the Netherlands asked potential employees to apply in 140 characters or less.

Utrecht-based Energize designed a web page that replicated the Twitter postbox. Candidates "tweeted" why they were the perfect person for the job. (The "tweets" were never actual public tweets; they were seen only by Energize's recruiters.)

At first blush, this might seem gimmicky — but remember, the ability to stay on-brand and professional within a very small posting space is an important skill set to have these days. Plus, it's a great time saver for the recruiter.

Speed "Dating"

In larger organizations, where each department might be looking for people, replicating existing social matchmaking techniques could prove helpful. This works especially well when you're looking for students who might be attracted to your company but aren't sure exactly what role they want to fill.

Here, you'll want to book out a bar or lounge and set up stations that replicate the departments seeking people. If the personality of your brand fits, you might even consider giving each station its own unique look and feel: a doctor's office, a kid's lemonade stand, and so on.

Start rotating candidates in seven-minute shifts. Remember: The goal isn't to hire people on the spot — only to determine if there's a match that might require follow-up. Give the person manning each station a sheet to record which candidates they are interested in; give a similar sheet to each candidate.

Unlike real speed dating, where only mutual matches are connected, interest by the station will be enough to contact the candidate for follow-up. When there also happens to be a mutual match, you can use this data as a way of prioritizing which candidates to contact first (or, given that they've expressed an interest in you as well, alter your negotiating technique).

If alcohol will be served during this event, be sure to provide taxi coupons so people can get home safely. This extra thoughtfulness will certainly stick in candidates' heads.

Video Questions

There's more to an applicant than the skills and background detailed on their resumé. If you're trying to build a more human organization, you'll need to see their mannerisms, how they respond on the fly, and the softer skills side of them.

The best way to do this is, of course, to have them come to your office and do an in-person interview. Some won't be local — needless to say, this cost would be out of reach for many organizations. This is why interviewing via video has become an important recruiting tool.

However, you'll want a more structured protocol for this than just occasional Skype video calls.

A platform called HireVue speeds up the process of hiring new employees. Rather than diving through resumés, hiring managers can watch applicants respond to a specific set of questions. These questions pop up on the applicant's screen for thirty seconds, then their webcam records their answer. Videos are then posted online for company recruiters to watch on-demand.

For larger organizations, one of the key advantages of this approach is in having a large pool of candidates answering the same question. This lets recruiters compare responses or use the video to refresh their memory before any in-person meetings.

Gamification

Play enough online role-playing games and you begin to wish for a world where candidates were ranked based on levels of adaptability, reasoning, and persuasion. This isn't to say you can't glean this from a candidate when they're in front of you, but it's much tougher to discern those soft skills from a resumé or online application.

Turns out, there are tools which can provide you with a measure of these skills — and using them can be fun for the candidates.

One such platform, ConnectCubed, gives players (applicants) a set of games that test spatial reasoning, ability to respond in rapid-fire situations, working memory, and personality type. Similar to brain-testing games like Lumosity, candidates are time-tested on skills with a score and "streak bonuses" (recognition for answering correctly in quick succession).

The software was initially developed for the financial trading industry in Asia. Since then, ConnectCubed has found that applicants tend to answer more questions through their program than through other similar recruiting tools, since ConnectCubed's games are engaging. You can customize the questions to uncover existing feelings about the brand and increase candidates' likelihood of wanting to accept a position.

The Marriott hotel chain used a Facebook game to try to fill some of the fifty thousand jobs they had open internationally.

This game, called My Marriott Hotel, was a Facebook app that tested candidates on their ability to manage a virtual hotel kitchen, including tasks like buying ingredients and equipment on tight budgets, serving guests, and hiring and training workers.

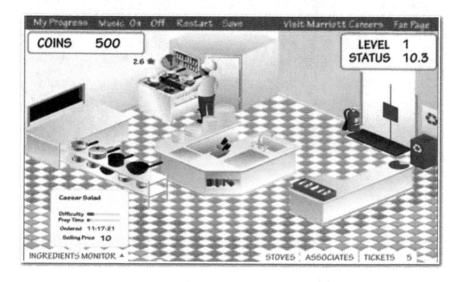

The game itself is adaptive — as in the real world, candidates boost their score when their operation turns a profit and lose points with poor customer service. Once the player has mastered the virtual kitchen, they can go on to play in other areas of the hotel. And, as a bonus, once the player achieves higher levels, they can post this success on their Facebook profile, providing additional brand awareness for the organization. You can watch a video of the game in action at *http://touchthebook.com/marriottgame.*

HACKING YOUR NEXT EMPLOYEE

In the hunt for a tech-savvy web designer, Ogilvy Brussels found a creative solution: They seeded files ostensibly disguised as Adobe's Creative Suite software through file-sharing websites like RapidShare, MediaFire, and DepositFiles.

Ogilvy bet that the types of people who'd try to download this expensive design software for free were designers who were out of work or low on money.

Rather than the software, though, the downloadable package contained a message reading: "If you're an unemployed web designer, you probably can't afford the crazy expensive application suite you need to work." A job offer was attached to the download — contingent, of course, on an interview and the usual recruiting stages.

OPEN SALARIES

Joel Gascoigne, CEO of social media tool Buffer, makes $151,800 per year. This isn't disclosing anything confidential. Gascoigne publishes his salary — and the salary of each Buffer employee — on his company's website.

His radical transparency has earned both accolades and criticism from the blogosphere. But one metric ticked dramatically up once he published the salaries: The number of people applying for jobs at Buffer doubled in one month.

It's not that the salaries are particularly generous — they're healthy but typical for a growing, well-funded tech start-up. Instead, it was the publication of the formula to arrive at the salaries which seems to have attracted attention. First, there is a base salary by position (customer service: $45k; designer: $60k). Then, a series of multipliers are added, depending on seniority, experience, and the location of work (no extra pay if you live in India; $22k extra if you're in San Francisco or Paris).

Buffer also offers employees a choice of more equity or more salary; if you choose salary, you get an additional ten thousand dollars but forfeit shares.

This kind of formula changes the way candidate negotiations take place. "The negotiating process is very alien to us at Buffer — because there is no negotiating," Gascoigne told the Quartz news service. "We have a really high focus on cultural fit to the point that if they didn't know about the formula before they applied, they probably wouldn't be a good fit. One bonus of transparency: You just search and learn. Generally, people are just really excited about the culture and they apply based on that.

"They [job candidates] have three separate interviews and one is focused on cultural fit. Then if we all agree we want the person to join the team, we make an offer letter with a forty-five-day trial period. One person recently replied: 'I would love to be on the team. I was thinking that that would be my salary.' He'd seen the formula and done the calculations himself."

This open-salaries idea is catching on. Other start-ups, like Groove and Customer.io, are emulating the system.

While the concept is working for Buffer, Gascoigne cautions that an all-or-nothing approach to transparency isn't the right way to get started. "Just do a little bit. Experiment with transparency in a small way. You don't have to go as far as posting everyone's salary on the blog. There's some cool things you could do. Every email between two or more people, any email in the team, you cc a list. We have a bunch of different lists. I'm emailing whom I'm going to meet. We've found some really incredible benefits of that. So share something that's not your most critical information. See how that feels — and just build from there."

BENEFITS

Thank Different

Money isn't the only way to provide an incentive for people to stick with your organization. Good teams, a fun and flexible environment, and great colleagues consistently rank highly in workplace studies.

A human organization needs to provide more than that, though. Gone are the days where flextime and work-at-home offerings are all that are needed to recruit and retain great people. You'll need to offer more. And smart companies are rethinking their benefits plans in an attempt to set themselves apart. Companies need to instill that flexibility and customization into the benefits packages they offer.

Some firms, like Google, offer a huge variety of perks. Another company, VoIP Supply, actually built an ice rink for their employees. It's tempting to pile on the offerings for everyone, but this can get expensive — and still not reach the right person.

To grow into a more human organization, you'll want to recognize that people aren't the same. One worker might want in-office dry cleaning pickup, another might need cheaper daycare for their children, while another might be retained because the lunches you offer are amazing.

For Jillian Walker, this kind of customization of benefits is a welcome emerging trend. "What organizations are moving to is based on allowances. 'Here's five grand, spend it on whatever you need within reason, and here's some structure to that. Or, we have, you know, five plans, this one's high [in] prescriptions, this one's high [in] massages or whatever, and here's how we are going to make our different plans work for where you are at in your life."

Luckily, this isn't work you need to do yourself. Push back against your current benefits-administration partner and ask them to develop a series of more flexible packages if they don't already offer them.

"What I'd say to them is 'I have fifty thousand dollars and here's what is important to my employees. I want them to have choice in their benefits package, and every single one has X amount of dollars toward this," explains Walker.

"I don't agree with just, like, the director of finance or director of IT spending a whole bunch of time on what does a benefits plan look like in order for an organization to be progressive. Use outsourced talent in order to get the job done."

Of course, not all organizations are of a size where it makes sense to bring in outside benefits administrators just to handle incentives. For those companies, self-service tools are bridging the gap. One such service, Uncover, lets you choose your company's perks from ten categories, including music, books, cleaning service, and others. When an employee goes above and beyond, you can reward them with something special. Employees choose which service they want and you're only charged for the perks they use. Even better, many of the offered perks can contribute to your organization's overall health — helping your employees stay up to date with online classes, promoting healthy lifestyles with gym memberships and health packages including yoga and Pilates, and even offering credit at Starbucks to keep employees feeling recognized. Uncover charges five dollars per month per employee and bills you for the perks only when they've been redeemed.

DON'T SEND THE WRONG MESSAGE

In 2002, when Tod owned his dot-com company, MindfulEye, the company was on a fierce growth curve. Programmers were pulling long hours and Tod decided to provide a space for people to relax. Like a lot of dot-com start-ups, a small room was designated as the "meditation/nap" room and employees were encouraged to take time out to rest their brains.

You continue to see this throughout the business world, though the most entertaining examples (foosball tables, racquetball on-site, etc.) seem to be in the fast-paced video game and software industries.

These efforts, well-intentioned as they are, send a very different message to employees than leaders sometimes mean. Leaders believe they're being generous in offering some space during work hours to zone out for a bit; many employees believe it sends the message "Sure, relax a bit, but whatever you do — don't leave the office!"

For Walker, these attempts at humanizing your organization can backfire.

"What is important to me is that employees have a life *outside* of work. I want them to come into an organization and thrive, create relationships, and technically 'rock it out.' But I also need them to have a rewarding home life," Walker says. "There's a way you can make services easier as a perk, without taking away the hours [employees] would normally spend at home. My preference ... is that employees don't live and breathe work. In order for you to be creative and innovative at work, your brain needs a break. If you only hang out with work people and you're only thinking about work all the time, your brain doesn't get that break in order to recharge and come back and add more value in the long term."

FLAT MODELS DONE RIGHT

The trend of "flat" organizations comes and goes in business. First seen among organizations trying to save money by removing middle management, this flattening trend has expanded to more specific models. Some of these models point the way to a more human, less bureaucratic company.

But even the most diehard communists might find Zappos' new flat corporate structure baffling.

In an attempt to squash its corporate structure, CEO Tony Hsieh has removed all management levels and removed everyone's titles.

It's not the first drastic move from the maverick leader — Zappos has offered "quit now" bonuses of two thousand dollars to new hires (it'll pay you to leave quickly if things aren't working out) — but it's one that many organizational consultants are watching closely.

The move, called "Holacracy" (the word is inspired by the Greek word "holon," which means "a whole that's part of a greater whole") was announced at an employee town hall. Hsieh replaced the traditional structure of managers and subordinates with four hundred "circles" — teams that work together on specific tasks.

The Zappos former manager leading the transition is John Bunch. He says: "One of the core principles is people taking personal accountability for their work. [Holacracy is] not leaderless. There are certainly people who hold a bigger scope of purpose for the organization than others. What it does do is distribute leadership into each role."

But removing managers has the risk of removing accountability. Without a clear sense of who's in charge, employees can become confused. And worse, your existing managers may find it difficult to understand their new role among a kitchen full of many chefs. Junior employees find themselves at the same decision-making level as people with more experience, which may not always benefit the organization.

Structure provides clarity and consistency. It gives people a sense of what they need to do to advance to higher pay levels.

A stronger model in play at project management firm 37signals sees people rotating management duties weekly.

Founder Jason Fried claims the new system "frees us from the often toxic labour-versus-management dynamic, in which neither party truly understands what it's like to be on the other side…. [It makes employees] more empathetic toward one another."

When considering a flatter structure, be sure you balance accountability with consistency.

Dan Pontefract, who leads the Transformation Office (an organizational culture-change consulting practice) of telco Telus, has developed the "flat army" model inside his organization. But unlike other flat models, his doesn't actually advocate for removing layers of management positions. "Flat is not devoid of managers and/or leaders. [To me it means] working on a level surface, not in a hierarchy for the sake of hierarchy…. Really, flat army is the chance for an organization to see that you can put human back into humanity inside of the organization while still achieving business results."

Pontefract conceived of the army metaphor in an homage to the medieval Latin term "armada" — which is simply a flotilla of vessels sailing together.

"A [truly flat army is what] I call an unobstructed flow of corporate commonality," he told us. "In essence, it is a behavioural statement. It says: 'Look, just don't tell people what to do by the end of the day because you need it done. Perhaps inject some humanity and ask, 'Do you have time?' 'Is this what you think is the right thing to do?'"

"We have these Fordism-to-Taylorism ways of a stopwatch clicking and trying to drive blood from a stone in our organization, because of what? Well, because of profit, of shareholder, of return, and so forth.

That is all going to stay forever — let's not kid ourselves. But can we do it in a context that allows the armada to sail together? I think we can and I think quite bluntly that is what organizations are missing."

It makes sense. But as to why companies aren't using the more human flat army model, Pontefract believes it's because of intertia on the part of leaders. "It is so much easier to quote 'command and control' than it is to connect and coordinate and be congratulative," he says. "If you're a parent, how much easier is it to yell at your kid to ... clean up [their] room — as opposed to, say, going through the behavioural modifications over a period of time to work through your child's effort, [and eventually they] want to help [make] your house clean and orderly? It's much easier to yell at your kid to tell them to make their bed. That is akin to what happens in the organization. It is much easier to tell someone what to do, treat them like a minion, or a number in the Enterprise Resource Planning (ERP) system and expect, because their wages are paid by you, you have hired them or you can fire them, that the threat and fear factor is ultimately the saving grace of how management should coordinate themselves. I find it abysmal."

Pontefract's book, *Flat Army: Creating a Connected and Engaged Organization*, outlines a more human approach to organizing your workforce to become more aligned. In it, he suggests a three-pronged approach: leadership, pervasive learning, and collaboration. In an interview with us, he sketched these out:

- **Leadership:** "I think a connected leader is one who gets the organization thinking like a tree. Trees have three key things — they have roots in the ground, they have a trunk, and they have foliage and ... beauty.... [As a leader,] you are deciding, you are delivering, you are analyzing data and what to do. That is when you are exploring new ideas. That is when you are adapting to situations. You are bettering a team and [yourself]."

- **Pervasive learning:** "As an organization of two hundred or two hundred thousand, we are always learning. What if [a small organization] had a learning paradigm that was equal parts formal, informal, and social, and what if some of those informal and social bits were things like coaching, mentoring, job rotations, and sending people out [in] the field to come back and report.

- **Collaboration:** "And then you add in those collaboration technologies. You have an opportunity to, regardless of where people live, demonstrate those behaviours of connected leadership and pervasive learning through things like microblogging, wikis, what have you. Don't start with the technology. Make a behavioural model that infuses those correct, I believe, and arguably altruistic behaviours that create that sense of commonality. And thus the point of the flat army."

But don't try to do it overnight. Pontefract warns that it's not a light switch; it is an ultra-marathon.

DOING "RESULTS FIRST" THE HUMAN WAY

Scientists have known for ages that we each have our own working rhythm. Some of us work best first thing in the morning; others are night owls who spark genius after the kids are put to bed.

How odd, then, that most organizations still insist on having all their workers show up at the same time (9:00 a.m.) and leave at the same time (5:00 p.m.). Sure, some companies proudly trumpet flextime as a benefit. However, if you dig deeper, you'll often discover this flextime is only flexible within a few hours' range.

It turns out the eight-hour workday structure we all work with today was developed as a way to make *factories* more efficient, not *people*.

Originally called the short-time movement, this concept was designed in the nineteenth century to break the unbearably long twelve- or fourteen-hour factory shifts common at the time. In 1810, Welsh politician Robert Owen called for a day with "eight hours labour, eight hours recreation, eight hours rest."

AVOIDING ATNA

If you have expectations that by flicking a switch you are going to change your culture, that you are going to move your engagement needle up, that people are all of a sudden going to be able to say nice things about your organization, that they are going to want to go above and beyond the call of duty, that they will ultimately want to retain their own team or their productivity levels to efforts and levels that are exceedingly above the average of Canada, U.S., western Europe, etc., you're blind. You need to capture this sense of culture by demonstrating over a period of time that you don't have what we call ATNA — all talk, no action.

And many organizations, many leaders, talk a really good game, but they fail because they might think [culture change] is a light switch or they might think it is just something that we have to say to the press or the analysts, that "people are our most important assets." Well, let's demonstrate it and let's understand that it might take you some time.

[Also,] you cannot have what we call "feel the dream syndrome." And that is, if you suggest to your organization, "Hey, we have built it, now you should come," that is not going to work either. That is sort of a gutless move because if you say to the organization, "Here it is, now you should join us," you haven't engaged with them through the process of reinvigorating and perhaps redefining what your organization is all about from a behavioural perspective. You can't just drop things on them and say, "Here is the new leadership model" or "Here is the new learning model" or "Start collaborating everyone" or "Here is a wiki."

The movement spread across Europe though it didn't truly pick up steam until 1914 when the Ford factories in America discovered that the eight-hour workday, in fact, improved worker productivity.

We've been stuck with it pretty much ever since.

Which isn't to say the eight-hour time block is the problem — the problem is that organizations have rigidly enforced a very specific eight hours (usually about 9:00 a.m. to 5:00 p.m.) regardless of their workers' own personal productivity patterns.

Think about your own organization — what matters more: the results of your workers or the time commitment of your workers? Likely the results. This is why some organizations are adopting a more human approach: ROWE — the "results-only work environment."

ROWE was originally developed at the Best Buy electronics chain. The idea behind it is remarkably simple: Head-office workers are compensated based on *what* they do, rather than *how long* it takes them to do it. Work begins to become a thing you do, rather than a place you do it. If your personal productivity zone is from 3:00 p.m. until 11:00 p.m., then that's when you should be working. And if you're more effective working on a laptop in a park, well, you should be able to do that.

The initial results were encouraging. All three key human resources metrics — productivity, retention, and morale — climbed dramatically. The company was said to have saved more than two million dollars over three years.

Other multinationals took notice of Best Buy's success and started implementing ROWE. The methodology's creators got a book deal, started keynoting conferences, and everything was coming up roses.

And then, all hell broke loose.

A new CEO took the helm at Best Buy and one of his first decisions was to kill the ROWE system. Hubert Joly explained his rationale in a newspaper commentary:

> This program was based on the premise that the right leadership style is always delegation. It operated on the assumption that if an employee's objectives were agreed to, the manager should always delegate to the employee how those objectives were met.

Well, anyone who has led a team knows that delegation is not always the most effective leadership style. If you delegate to me the job of building a brick wall, you will be disappointed in the result! Depending on the skill and will of the individual, the right leadership style may be coaching, motivating, or directing, rather than delegating. A leader has to pick the right style of leadership for each employee, and it is not one-size-fits-all, as the ROWE program would have suggested.

The decision to drop ROWE sent shock waves across the business media, and the program's creators (former Best Buy managers Cali Ressler and Jody Thompson) lashed out:

> [This new] management obviously favours managing schedules over managing performance — the stronghold of outdated thinking became the weed that choked the evolution of the most enviable, productive, attractive, and globally-forward workforce of the future.... They are more concerned with having leadership excel at monitoring the hallways, rather than building a leadership team that excels at defining clear, measurable results, and holding people accountable for achieving those results. While we agree that Best Buy must take drastic measures to turn their business around, moving back to a twentieth century, paternalistic "command and control" environment is most certainly not the answer ...

Joly's decision exemplifies the Theory X style of management. (Again, Theory X states that employees are generally lazy and the best way to motivate them is through tight supervision and pervasive threats of dismissal.)

Best Buy wasn't the first organization to drop a more flexible workplace. Yahoo's newly minted chief executive, Marissa Mayer, cancelled the company's widespread telecommuting program. Other organizations quietly scaled back similar workplace innovations.

So, what happened?

Simply, management tried to do too much, too fast.

In implementing a ROWE-based system, many organizations forced both time and location displacement into the mix — allowing people to both change the time of their work and the location of their work.

The fact is, some organizations simply need people in the office to make things work better — a fact Best Buy's spokesperson acknowledged when ROWE was dropped: "Bottom line, it's 'all hands on deck' at Best Buy and that means having employees in the office as much as possible to collaborate and connect on ways to improve our business."

Sadly, Best Buy was right in this aspect — despite technological advances in telecommuting, shared documents, and collaborative online meetings, productivity increases when colleagues physically share the same space.

(As a side note: While Tod and Mark were working on this book, they tripled their writing output when they were together for a few days in the same city.)

ROWE's primary foundations are built on trust — trusting employees to get a list of assigned work at a mutually agreed deadline.

The thing about trust is that it's best fostered in person, looking someone in the eye, spending time physically in the same space.

So while location displacement was flawed, time displacement absolutely works.

Given the opportunity to choose their working hours, most employees will still plan their day around a basic daytime structure. Some might come in at 6:00 a.m. and others might not roll in until noon, though in almost all circumstances there exist a common few hours. This is the perfect time for midday meetings or other processes where in-person attendance is important.

Implementing a Human "Results-First" Methodology in Your Workplace

1. **Can you do it at all?** Some corporate cultures just don't fit into a system that prefers tasks accomplished over

hours spent. This kind of methodology might be a hard sell to government groups or very large enterprises.

2. **Create a champion team.** If you expect buy-in from the trenches, put the people in the trenches in charge. Ask who'd like to volunteer to be on a champion team that would implement the plan. You'll want no more than six people who represent a variety of business functions and seniority. Don't be afraid to put a new hire on the team, as they might bring valuable experience from a previous results-first organization.

3. **Poll your people.** You'll have to figure out what time overlaps will exist if you launch this plan. Ask your people what time slots they'd prefer to work in, and assure them that this is only for general planning and, of course, they'll be able to move that time around when circumstances warrant.

4. **Pilot it.** If you have separate office locations or strongly siloed units, pilot the project for at least three months in a single location. This will give you a heads-up on potential issues or culture conflict. Keep the numbers down to fewer than a hundred people so that the next phase (measure human metrics) is manageable. Ensure that the managers in the pilot project have the skills to set clear output objectives with their teams. (This soft skill doesn't come easily to many executives, who are used to valuing people for their time, not their results.)

5. **Measure human metrics.** At the end of the pilot project, measure (by way of an anonymous online survey) the human metrics of the project — use simple language like "Are you generally happier at work?" or "Do you feel you're getting more done now than before?"

6. **Hold a town hall meeting.** Remember, workers will buy into the plan much more if they help create it. Once you've piloted a results-first environment, call a company-wide town hall, outline what happened in the pilot, present the results of the survey, and ask for feedback. At the end of the meeting, ask the group whether they believe you should implement it to a wider group. If the consensus is no, don't do it!

7. **Upgrade manager skills.** If you've decided to roll out a results-first environment organization-wide, present team leaders with the opportunity to develop stronger skill sets in results-based project management. This investment will go a long way to ensuring the project's success.

8. **Measure, measure, measure.** At least annually, measure the human metrics again to make sure your people are happier with this system than with the previous one, what areas you need to bulk up on, and — most importantly — if the project is, indeed, delivering stronger business results.

GAMIFYING GOALS

Thomas Watson Sr., the founder of IBM, had an effective, if peculiar, way of rewarding employees for good performance. He would walk around the assembly line and, when he saw someone who deserved recognition, he'd stop and write out a cheque for five dollars or more. Many people would frame the cheque instead of cashing it.

These days, some services are emerging to help reward the people who work in your organization.

Do a web search for "team project management" and you'll find hundreds of web services — everything from full task-lists like those offered by Asana to deeper full-project systems. They all have their pros and cons, even though few of these project management tools incorporate the human experience of reward.

While clicking a "completed" tick-box surges a little dopamine through the brain, using these project management systems often ends up just becoming one more thing to do.

A more human approach, of course, is to make the completion of tasks a fun experience — a reward unto itself.

And, to be sure, different systems have indeed tried to "gamify" (adding video game-like functions like achievements, levelling up, XP points, and so on) project management to encourage teams to work together.

Now let's look at the record.

These systems use digital rewards as perks to encourage task completion. However, these individual one-offs, in fact, produce the opposite effect. Short-term boosts in productivity are realized and then engagement settles back to former levels once the novelty of competing for low-value gift cards (or whatever the perks offered are) wears thin.

As well, these systems (let's call them Gamification 1.0) are all designed around the individual and not the team. While the concept of having your employees compete to be more productive seems tempting, the reality is that this fosters distrust among colleagues and business units. ("Do they really need that report for their project, or is it so their team can win this week?")

A more human approach is to think broadly about your organization's overall goals and incorporate those business goals into any gamification system you plan to implement. After all, you want to encourage more than task completion — you want to reward the complete skill-mastery life cycle — learning new skills, using them, and passing them onto others.

For instance, is ongoing skills training an important part of your mission? (If not, make it so.) Then tasks related to that goal should be included in any task-reward program you take on. And people should be rewarded without being in competition with each other.

GAMIFYING THE WRONG WAY

GAMIFICATION 1.0 PERKS	ACTUAL RESULT
Few valuable prizes (vacation, bonus)	Top performers consistently win. Incentive to both excel and undermine others. Dog eat dog.
Many trivial prizes (badge for login, update profile picture)	Incents engagement with system. Reduces overall productivity as people focus on badges over work.
Leaderboards tracking running totals (sales closed, hours clocked)	Rewards seniority. Moving up difficult without attrition or productivity decrease of higher-ranked staff. Both actions reduce aggregate productivity.

Table from propstoyou.com

Luckily, some smarter systems are showing up — call them Gamification 2.0.

PropsToYou operates like a role-playing game in which registering a completed task gains the employee "skill points" which are then logged on their own profile page. This system, and ones like it, capitalize on some very human traits.

1. **Connection to the bigger picture:** Workers are rewarded for their role in reaching broader organizational goals like mentoring others, learning new skills that benefit the company, and helping a colleague. These soft tasks provide long-term benefit to an organization and any task-reward system you implement needs a way to track them.

2. **The fun of surprise:** Managers can place random "Easter eggs" into the project so that employees occasionally get surprise rewards. (Behavioural science has proven that unexpected rewards based on secret criteria keep people

focused on their real work instead of on trying to figure out how to game the system.)

3. **Friendly "competition" ritual:** While not competing directly (e.g., your win won't prevent a colleague from also winning), team members will be able to see their progress on a results board, which is unveiled at a specific time each week. This creates an opportunity for a team-wide event to see where people are placed.

4. **Competing with yourself:** PropsToYou tracks your individual performance over time, giving each person a personal-best bar to aspire to beat. Again, these points can be driven from completion of specific tasks or working toward whole-organization goals.

5. **Exposed public reputation:** Part of eBay's success is its public reputation system, where everyone can see how trusted a seller or buyer is. Similarly, workers participating in smart, human-based task gamification will be able to track the productivity and effectiveness of their colleagues. This reputation is based, first and foremost, on consistency. (This is very different from the Gamification 1.0 goal-based games that would see huge productivity gains while the game was running, followed by a crash after scores stopped being tabulated.)

6. **Different strokes for different folks:** The awards in PropsToYou are neither arbitrary nor biased, and everyone is on the same field. The frequency of award automatically adjusts to the level of the recipient. New employees get frequent yet trivial encouragement (this does not appear in their permanent game profile) while senior staff receive occasional yet deeply meaningful praise (permanent personal congratulations in the game system written by their project leader).

Systems like these provide a few hidden benefits:

- **Automated annual reviews:** Throughout the year, the employee's work is graded by their peers and shown online to their managers. This should provide for an annual review with no surprises to the employee.

- **Early-warning system:** When your workers' efficiency is being tracked by their colleagues each week, you end up with a very effective bellwether for poorly performing team members. You'll know within a couple of weeks if someone is starting to slip on their productivity.

- **Fairer employee recognition:** Many well-meaning organizations implement employee recognition programs to single out a few people who've excelled in their team. Often the criteria for winning this award isn't well known. By using the metrics delivered from a goal-game system, everyone will agree that the colleague in question did, indeed, perform well.

START WITH THE RIGHT FOUNDATION

Dan Pontefract warns that rushing in with technology first, though, can spell disaster.

"To gamify leadership before you have ultimately created the defining behaviours and expectations is sort of like [putting the] cart before the horse," he told us. "So for an organization to just drop a technology in and gamify the leadership model, I am not sure that is the correct approach. Trust me, I am 'Dan two-point-oh.' I will put any type of technology into the hands of people to make it easier for them to do their jobs, to connect, to lead, etc. But I would not start with it."

Notably, in his book *Flat Army: Creating a Connected and Engaged Organization*, it's not until chapter ten of thirteen that he discusses technology. The first nine chapters are about the behaviours of leading, of organizational change, and engagement.

REWARD THE RIGHT THINGS

One trap to make sure you don't fall into is rewarding the wrong things in your organization. If your reward system is based on things like increased time spent at work or increased gross revenue (without an eye to actual profitability), your team members will work toward those goals, not toward what might be the most productive.

In his groundbreaking book *The 360 Degree Leader: Developing Your Influence from Anywhere in the Organization*, John C. Maxwell pens this story:

> A man was enjoying an afternoon in a small fishing boat on a peaceful lake. He fished as he munched on a chocolate bar. The weather was perfect, his cellphone was turned off and all he could think about was how happy he was.

Just then he spotted a snake in the water with a frog in its mouth. He felt sorry for the frog, so he scooped up the snake with his landing net, took the frog out of its mouth, and tossed it to safety. Then he felt sorry for the snake. He broke off a piece of his chocolate bar, gave it to the snake, and placed it back in the water, where it swam away.

There, he thought. The frog is happy, the snake is happy, and now I'm happy again. This is great. He cast his line back into the water and then settled back again.

A few minutes later, he heard a bump on the side of the boat. He looked over the side, and there was the snake again. This time it had two frogs in [its] mouth!

Maxwell's moral is: Be careful what you reward, because what gets rewarded gets done.

WHY YOUNG EMPLOYEES QUIT

Forget the recession — the biggest challenge companies will face in the next five years is yet to come: a mass exodus of employees from the workforce. Baby boomers have already begun retiring en masse and scant few organizations have any kind of succession plan in place to recruit and groom future leaders.

It's not like they haven't tried. Managers have hired legions of so-called Generation Y workers to fill offices, only to watch in disbelief and confusion as scores walk out the back door as easily as they came in the front. Understanding the fickle needs of workers in their twenties is a moving target, and indicators are emerging pointing to why young workers hit the bricks.

- **They feel mistrusted.** Especially true for your younger employees born to Generation X parents between 1980 and 1990 (who gave them unprecedented levels of trust and room off-leash as compared to their own baby-boomer parents), today's workforce expects to be trusted in all aspects of their life, including on the job. Misguided attempts at increasing productivity, like blocking Facebook and instant-messenger programs, scream "We don't trust you!" to this group of workers. After all, you don't block the telephone in case your employees make personal calls. To your employees today, blocking other modes of communication like social networking sites amounts to the same thing.

- **They feel like a cog.** Employees want to feel like a part of the team from day one, not like it's something they have to earn after months of employment. If you're holding your new workers back from participating in a project simply because they haven't cleared their three-month probation, you are, in essence, telling them that they were hired for their ability to fill a chair, not to play a valued role in a firm. Remember, this generation was told by their parents that they can do anything they set their mind to. Holding them back from that potential in the workplace will confuse and eventually frustrate your workers.

- **You give them annual reviews.** In past generations, workers were evaluated once per year in a horribly demoralizing session known as The Annual Review. This review was, essentially, the recitation of a list of things an employee did wrong in the previous 365 days, coupled with an opportunity for them to beg for a raise. It doesn't work any more. Today, workers expect instant feedback — people can take criticism, as long as it's justified, immediate, and gives them a fair opportunity to correct the problem. Corrections should happen when needed, not held for a year-end meeting, and should start with the words: "Let me know how I can help support you better so this doesn't happen again."

- **Your technology sucks.** Remember as well that your younger employees simply do not know a world without immediate access to information like the Internet and email. And yet, so many corporate offices still slog by on computers that groan and chug slowly when asked to perform basic tasks like opening a spreadsheet or launching a web browser. Your technology must at least keep pace with the computers this generation uses at home. This doesn't necessarily mean buying the latest bleeding-edge turbo-machines, though it also doesn't mean a patched-up computer from the secretary pool, either. (Um, you still have a secretary pool?!)

- **You don't give them unstructured time.** Often, companies attempt to increase worker output by restricting the time available for water-cooler chat, coffee breaks, and so on. First, eliminate scheduled breaks entirely. Let them take breaks when they feel they need to. Paradoxically, given this level of trust, engaged workers will return the favour in spades by devoting extra time at work, often unpaid. This time gives them the chance to cross-pollinate ideas across projects or departments, share news between divisions, and otherwise break down the traditional "silos" that hamper an organization's agility. Remember, this informal connection time is the way they were taught to work in school — group projects, not individual reports. Don't worry, you'll be able to spot the abusers of this generosity clearly.

    You can audit your own organization's ability to retain today's workers. Start with the easiest three:

1. Are you rewarding, not just encouraging, the sharing of information and ideas across the company?

2. Do you have updated computers and have a "just
don't go overboard" policy when it comes to your
workers using websites like Facebook and Twitter?

3. Are employees in the first three months of employment involved in important and exciting projects?

Now that economic recovery is ahead, the days of workers competing for jobs will once again sunset. Soon enough, they'll be back in
the driver's seat. If your company isn't prepared to respect the needs of
today's workforce, you may find yourself struggling for relevance in the
new economy.

THE NEW OPEN-PLAN WORKSPACE

A couple of decades ago, organizational psychologists began claiming
that the private-office structure of most workspaces — with employees
assigned individual closed-door offices — should be broken down and
everyone made to sit in a single large space. This, they said, would increase
communication among people in the room.

They were right. It dramatically increased communication. Problem
is, the communication was mostly the noise of people making calls,
shouting over to a colleague's desk, holding impromptu meetings in
cubicles, and so on.

So employees in open-plan workplaces developed their own ways of
getting some quiet brain time — they'd wear headphones or put "Do not
talk to me" ball caps on their heads. And in no time, everyone was sitting
again in their own private, if imaginary, closed-door offices. Hardly a
human approach.

We now know that open-plan offices are terribly distracting. The
International Management Facility Association, which helps members
plan office spaces, believes that seven out of ten U.S. employees now

work under such conditions — conditions that aren't helping them get much work done. The design firm Gensler discovered people who work in open-plan offices spend only half their time at work in deep focus. The rest they spend collaborating with colleagues, socializing, and doing other things. And when they need to get real work done, they move to — wait for it — closed-door meeting spaces.

Work requires concentration, especially work in today's knowledge economy. Microsoft knew that during its more successful era two decades ago; it gave nearly each programmer, regardless of seniority, their own private office in which to program. These spaces helped them focus (sometimes obsessively so — stories of programmers who would eat only flat food that could be slipped under their door began to make the rounds in the tech community).

This isn't to say that a return to everyone having their own private office is the solution either.

A human organization should replicate comfortable surroundings, like those in the home environment, with different rooms serving different functions: one for eating, one for sleeping, one for working, one for relaxing, one for hobbies, and so on.

Besides the functional tasks, a human organization needs to recognize that there are different types of work personalities — introverts, extroverts, leaders, followers, and others.

This is something Google understands. The company's director of global design, Christopher Coleman, says, "We found that [our employees] need a lot of diversity. There are so many ways to work — as a team, solo — and so many kinds of workers, from introverts to extroverts and so on. We create many different places so people can be as productive as possible — from formal and informal conference rooms to open spaces to stretching and yoga areas and gyms."

Gensler's head of workplace design, Janet Pogue, believes workplaces should create a mix of spaces, broken down by the type of activity occurring there.

- **Concentrate:** Workers need brain time, and they can't get that with a phone that won't stop ringing. Pogue says *some* kind of personal space employees can retreat to, even one that doesn't necessarily have walls, is a critical component of a healthy and human workplace.

- **Collaborate:** Just because people sit together doesn't mean they collaborate. Often, people's seating is assigned by department or corporate rank and not by functional task groups. The people who need to meet to get things done need an informal, relaxed space for this collaborative work.

- **Learn:** Pogue believes that the idea of a dedicated space set aside for learning — both classroom-style or less formal, smaller spaces — is often overlooked. These spaces should have technology in place for this kind of work.

- **Socialize:** You don't want to foster an environment where people are chatting all the time, in every space. By setting aside a specific area for socializing, people still get the opportunity to pick up news from other parts of the organization. One way of structuring this, says Pogue, is to take people's individual printers away and make them get their print jobs from a common area.

THE POWER OF SCENT

Considering most of us spend more than a third of our day at work, it's surprising that we haven't made these spaces more comfortable — especially given the scientific research which proves the use of subtle scents can have a positive impact on productivity.

- The scent of peppermint and that of rosemary are both said to increase concentration.

- A 2008 study published in the *Journal of Agricultural and Food Chemistry* found the mere smell of coffee kick-starts the brain, reducing the stress resulting from lack of sleep.

- A study of elementary school teachers in Taiwan found that the scent of bergamot (an orange-like fruit) reduced their heart rate and blood pressure — the more stressed they were, the better the scent worked. (Interestingly, the study found this mood effect worked when the oil was applied to the skin and not inhaled, further suggesting a real biological, and not just perceived, effect.)

Little wonder that casinos — which pour millions into researching the science of encouraging people to linger longer in their spaces — pump custom-blended aromatherapy compounds into their air system. This is why the Westin hotel chain developed its own white tea aromatherapy scent, with which it fills its lobbies and infuses its soaps and shampoos. The hotel sells candles, oils, and even a home version of their ScentWave diffusion system.

There's more:

- A line of peppermint-scented pencils (called Smencils) has been developed, made from sheets of newspaper rather than wood. The paper is tightly rolled around the graphite cores, then the whole pencil is soaked in a specially crafted peppermint-scented mixture. Once dry, the pencils are stored in a tube which can retain their scent for up to two years.

- Brazilian ad agency GrupoFourMidio designed scented parking receipts after they noticed that drivers often put the receipts in their mouths while looking for a parking space. The scent was related to an advertisement on the receipt, opening up new ad venues for food- or perfume-based brands.

- Working with a Singapore-based perfume maker, the global creative agency JWT created a set of scents personalized to individual residents of nursing homes. With names like Bedtime Stories, Mom's Cooking, Prayer, and School Days, the scents were designed to help people with dementia remember memories from their past and boost their mood.

And yet, despite the established research around the power of scent to alter our mood and productivity levels, businesses seem wary of exploiting scents in the workplace.

Indeed, there's something of a backlash against scents in the workplace.

Recently, a Detroit city worker filed a lawsuit complaining that a co-worker's perfume made it difficult for her to do her job. The city fought the case, saying there was no medical proof that she wasn't able to work. Nevertheless, a court agreed with the worker and forced the city to make three of its buildings 100 percent scent free.

While there's no federal legislation surrounding a scent-free work-place, some businesses are finding themselves caught in an ever-widening definition of a "safe and healthy" workplace. (One expert — Jan Chappel, senior technical specialist for the Canadian Centre for Occupational Health and Safety — believes up to a third of Canadian businesses have a no-cologne policy at work.) Indeed, environmental sensitivity is considered a disability in Ontario's Human Rights Code, though — contrary to common belief — scent sensitivities aren't considered disabling under the code. The provincial human rights commission has only ever received two complaints about scent sensitivity and both were resolved privately.

Let's be clear. Sitting beside someone who bathes in their cologne isn't much fun. And for people who have a sensitivity to strong odours, it can absolutely prove to be a health issue.

There's a difference between an overpowering smell and barely detectible overtones of an uplifting scent. Far too few businesses have tried the latter, and it's a shame.

THE WRONG WAY

In what surely is the worst possible way to terminate a group of employees, Patch, the failing "hyperlocal" news site launched in 2007, laid off two-thirds of its staff in January 2014 via — wait for it — a mass conference call.

In a disturbingly upbeat tone, Patch's COO (not even the CEO or the affected employees' direct manager), Leigh Zarelli Lewis, read out into the speakerphone a statement which included this:

> Patch is being restructured in connection with the creation of the joint venture with Hale Global.... Unfortunately, your role has been eliminated and you will no longer have a role at Patch and today will be your last day of employment with the company.

She followed up by reciting some administrivia and told the hundreds of newly fired workers on the call at what time they had to stop using their company laptops.

And then she chirped, "Thank you again and, um, best of luck."
Click.
The entire call lasted less than two minutes.
Never do this.
Ever.

ON THE HORIZON

Vigo Drowsiness Detector

Sometimes, team members' energy levels deplete quickly — and often, by the time they're aware of it, their productivity level is already shot for the day. Some new technologies are trying to combat that and alert workers to moments when they might want to take a break.

Vigo is a wearable headset sensor that picks up on when someone gets drowsy and offers real-time data on their alertness. It looks like a cellphone Bluetooth headset and comes with a motion detector that can monitor the wearer's eye blinks. Up to twenty data points calculated from those blinks are used to determine the person's mental energy level, providing notifications to the device suggesting when that person probably needs a break.

Different notification levels can be set, depending on the worker's condition — anything from a discreet vibration to a flashing light on their cellphone right through to the playing of a high-energy song from their computer's music application. The device can also track their performance over time to see when their peak concentration time is.

And since Vigo behaves like a Bluetooth device, you can even take calls on it.

Be sure to check it out at *http://touchthebook.com/vigo*

Breather — Instant Workspaces

Many organizations offer off-site working for their employees, freeing people from their desks. To date, there really have been only two models for this off-site work — home-ish and work-ish. Home-related spaces include a separate bedroom or even a nearby coffee shop. Work-related spaces usually involve renting a monthly shared office space in a work centre.

These models offer great options for people who like to work in either space. To date there hasn't been anything in between: the informality of working from home combined with a quiet business-appropriate space without monthly lease commitments.

That's where Montreal-based Breather is filling the gap.

Using the company's mobile app, people can search for nearby private spaces that are suitable for working — quiet, with a desk and chair, and with Wi-Fi access — and can be used in a pinch for a last-minute client presentation or prospect meeting. The price is around twenty dollars per hour.

Think of it like Airbnb for the business crowd. Users rate the room quality (was it quiet and comfortable?), and room owners rate the guests (did they clean up after they left?). Poor ratings on either side get that party blocked from Breather's network. The spaces themselves are largely self-running — web-programmable door locks let space owners provide access to specific guests at their booking time. Outside of those times, the lock won't work.

You can read more about Julien's project at *http://touchthebook. com/breather*

Buoy — Move While Working

The number of ergonomic chairs sold for workplaces is huge. However, most of these devices simply support your limbs in a more comfortable position, without necessarily encouraging you to move around. One product under development, the Buoy, seeks to encourage movement while working. The Buoy is, essentially, a short, cylindrical stool that can swivel, tilt, and move up and down. More importantly, it remains somewhat off balance, owing to its rounded bottom. When workers sit on it, they need to shift their position on the stool to maintain balance. At just twenty pounds, it's easy to move around to different rooms and meeting spaces. You can match Buoy to your workspace. It's available in six colours and twenty-five seat-fabric options.

Have a look at *http://touchthebook.com/buoy*

TOUCHPOINTS: FIVE HR TAKEAWAYS

 Technology has changed the way we promote job opportunities, seek them out, and apply for them. It's also driven a shift in culture, one that demands more authenticity, openness, and transparency. Watch closely for more upcoming changes in human behaviours, facilitated by advancements in technology.

 Employee acquisition and retention have changed significantly over recent years. Expect even more interest in innovation as digital natives become the leaders, and the next digitally-engaged generation looks for work.

 There are many innovative and even crazy new ideas in the world of organizational structure and HR management. Not all will work for your organization. There's plenty of information online about each idea. Seek them out and see if variations of any may be a fit.

 People shouldn't have to wait for periodic performance reviews. They'll be much happier to get productive feedback on an ongoing basis and especially when it's connected to a recent event.

 People want to feel both valued and appreciated. That means more than just a handsome paycheque. It means speaking with them and dealing with them in a human way. If doing that doesn't come naturally to you, delegate to someone on your team who is better equipped, and learn from them.

CHAPTER 10

LEGAL

"Cease and desis—"..? For god's sake, Pemberton, leave the lawyers out of it
and just *tell* me to stop cracking my knuckles in meetings.

You won't find a lot of humanity in the legal department of your organization. Not that the people who work there aren't caring, sensitive folks — it's just that the legal system has its own arcane, depersonalized language.

This unfortunate legal lexicon is why human resources people use clinically cold language like, "I am required to inform you that your employment is terminated, effective immediately," when they fire someone, instead of a simpler and more human, "I have some bad news, June. Your employment is ending today." Same message — just as direct. And, more human.

Language and tone are such important parts of developing into a more human organization. The question becomes, how can you maintain this softer voice without losing important legal messaging?

CONSIDER THE SOFTBALL

While most legal executives opt for a strong-worded tone, American patent and trademark attorney Anton Hopen has become skilled at adding human nuance to the unfortunate necessity of cease-and-desist (C&D) letters.

His firm, Smith and Hopen, calls the standard form of this letter that you've probably seen the "Furious Demand" letter. It's meant to strike fear into the opposing party. "The undersigned attorney is seemingly outraged that the alleged infringer is still breathing," lead litigator Ron Smith explains. "The Furious Demand is heavy on threats but light on facts. All infringement is egregious, knowing, and malicious. The letter will invariably demand:

- an immediate halt to all business operations involving the alleged infringement;

- immediate destruction of the allegedly offending articles or equipment in support of the infringement;

- the identity of all customers that bought the infringing article;

- the total number of infringing articles sold;

- advisement of the profit margin for each article and the total profits made; and

- an opportunity to admit infringement and grovel for a settlement.

This seems to be the default tone for many legal executives, drummed into them at law school to go fast and go hard. It's hardly human. It ends up alienating the opposing party and leaving a bad taste in everyone's mouth.

Worse, says Hopen, the Furious Demand is often the product of a junior lawyer. "The less experienced attorneys always take the hard-ball approach. You almost know that you are dealing with somebody who is less experienced and probably less self-confident when there is a lot of bravado. The typical demand letter that you receive in my area will be 'You have to stop everything you are doing, you have to give us all your confidential books, you have to do an accounting of all the damages you owe us, and we reserve all rights to sue you.

"Nobody responds to that. It's such an absurd thing to even request. So the thing about it is, the person that you impose this on may be the same person that you need a favour from some day later on."

Indeed, not every situation calls for the Furious Demand. In fact, most probably don't.

An example: In 2005, Arizona student Jose Avila just wanted to make furniture. He didn't have a lot of money and discovered that FedEx boxes were quite sturdy and, assembled the right way, could support a lot of weight. He took some photos of his new "couch" and posted them online. FedEx's lawyers sent him a Furious-style cease-and-desist.

Decades ago, trademark infringement case law was open-and-shut. If someone infringed on your trademark, you got them to stop. In today's world where everyone has access to a digital bullhorn (Avila went on national television, no less) a knee-jerk C&D letter may not be the most advisable approach.

Think about what the photo of Avila lying on a couch made of a few dozen FedEx boxes visually communicated: These boxes are strong! And if they're strong enough for a college student to lie on without them even bending, then they're probably solid enough for you to ship things in.

FedEx missed a massive opportunity here, and simply because they opted for the overly legal — not human — solution.

There are plenty of similar examples:

- In 1998, David Sams registered the domain *veronica.org* for his infant daughter. Archie Comics sent him a C&D. After Sams went on national television, the company quietly backed down.

- A year earlier, a twelve-year-old who was known by the nickname "Pokey" received *pokey.org* as a birthday present. Prema Toy Co., which owns the rights to the characters Gumby and Pokey, sent him a C&D. The matter was dropped only when the original creator of the Pokey the Horse character petitioned the company to calm down.

- In 1999, when toy collector Gus Lopez received a C&D letter from Toys R Us for using the domain name *toysrgus.com* to showcase his collection, Lopez replaced the entire website with the takedown letter, the e-mail address of the lawyer who sent it, and a full background on the issue.

After defending more than 1,500 patents and 1,200 federal trademark filings, Hopen now often relies on a more human approach he calls the Softball Demand. An example the firm uses:

Dear Mr. Jones:

It has come to our attention that your ABC-brand widget has several features that appear to be claimed by our client's patent (enclosed). Our client has advised us that XYZ Corporation enjoys a long-standing reputation in the industry as a reputable and conscientious business. Thus, we presume XYZ Corporation was unaware of the existence of our client's patent. However, we believed it prudent for XYZ Corporation to be aware of the patent as soon as we learned of this situation. From a preliminary review, we are inclined to believe the ABC-brand widget infringes on the patent claims. However, we would appreciate your thoughts on this matter. Please feel free to contact us at your convenience. We look forward to hearing from you.

This more human approach assumes that the violation was simply an oversight and seeks the opposing party's *thoughts*, rather than their immediate compliance. Note that harsh words like "infringement" aren't used at any time in the Softball Demand. With this approach, you maintain a working relationship with the other party — after all, your competitor or opponent today might easily become your business partner tomorrow in these fast-paced times.

That said, if you need to word things strongly, a more human approach is to use the Bad News First method.

"One of my clients would copy me on emails where he was threatened [with] litigation," recalls Hopen. "We are talking very, very big corporations here. This is CEO to CEO with their general counsel copied on it too… 'Here are all of the grievances I have; here are all of the problems that I have.' And when someone is giving you the third degree, you are going to read every single word. You are not going to blow it off. But then my client would always end on this great positive note, always end on this upswing. And it was just like magic.

"He'd say something like 'I recognize this may not be what you wanted to hear, however I see an opportunity here.' Never present a problem without offering a solution."

EMBRACE THE UNOFFICIALS

And Now, the Right Way

When author Patrick Wensink's satirical novel *Broken Piano for President* was published he wasn't expecting any controversy over its cover design.

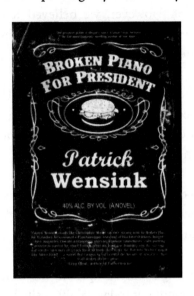

The cover, inspired by old-time saloon-era art, bore a striking resemblance to the label of Jack Daniel's Tennessee Whiskey.

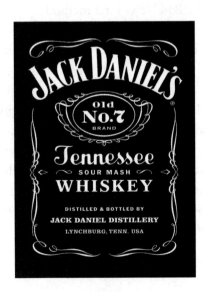

Jack Daniel's felt a legal response was necessary — and they were right. And, they approached it with a human attitude that made all the difference.

> We are certainly flattered by your affection for the brand, but while we can appreciate the pop culture appeal of Jack Daniel's, we also have to be diligent to ensure that the Jack Daniel's trademarks are used correctly. Given the brand's popularity, it will probably come as no surprise that we come across designs like this on a regular basis. What may not be so apparent, however, is that if we allow uses like this one, we run the very real risk that our trademark will be weakened. As a fan of the brand, I'm sure that is not something you intended or would want to see happen....
>
> In order to resolve this matter, because you are both a Louisville 'neighbour' and a fan of the brand, we simply request that you change the cover design when the book is reprinted. If you would be willing to change the design sooner than that (including on the digital version), we would be willing to contribute a reasonable amount toward the costs of doing so.

The letter went viral and for all the right reasons.

The lesson is clear — when somebody does something amazing and unofficial with your brand, you should embrace them, not threaten them.

Ask First

Digital culture is a strange animal for some organizations. In fact, it seems the organizations that struggle most with social networking are hamstrung by digital engagement and relationship building. They fail to realize that social etiquette itself hasn't changed, just the places where it's practised have.

At a conference in 2011, members of Canada's National Capital Commission (NCC) itemized a number of fascinating ways they were using videos, video booths, social media news releases, and social networks to promote various events and activate the public to produce content for those events. They also admitted to having bigger hopes than they were able to realize, including some failed attempts to create viral videos.

The list was interesting, though not nearly as attention-getting as one action the presenters seemed particularly pleased about.

They related the story of wanting to appropriate a Twitter handle similar to a Canadian trademark they had registered for the annual Winterlude event. The @Winterlude Twitter account they wanted was held by another individual, possibly in the United States.

This NCC's legal team worked with Twitter to appropriate the account. It took a week.

The air in the conference room seemed to vanish in an instant.

Mark was at the conference. He asked if the NCC had approached the account holder first to see if the two parties could arrive at an amiable agreement to transfer control of the account. They hadn't. In fact, the nature of the response suggested that was never an option for the organization. Instead, the NCC exerted their authority as Canadian trademark holders and went directly to Twitter.

The presenters gave no indication the previous account holder was doing anything that presented a reputation risk to the NCC or Winterlude. Simply put, the account holder happened to be using a handle they wanted and had legal claim to in Canada.

The PR professional sitting next to Mark was equally stunned. She piped in to the conversation, telling a similar story with a different twist.

BE A GOOD NETIZEN. BE COLLABORATIVE, CO-OPERATIVE, AND OPERATE WITH DIGITAL GRACE. PLAY WITH GOOD KARMA. IT COULD HELP YOU WHEN YOU MOST NEED IT.

The organization she worked for at the time had wanted to open a LinkedIn group. It turns out the name they wanted was already in use. So, she sent the group owner a note asking if the owner would consider coming to an arrangement to share or transfer control of the group. Not only did the existing owner agree, she offered to do so without compensation.

How you present yourself and conduct your business says a lot about your values and culture — this is true of individuals and organizations, both online and off.

A HUMAN SOCIAL MEDIA POLICY

Your legal department won't just be handling C&D letters, of course. It'll be involved in preparing human resources policies and other internal documents.

Unfortunately, it seems to be a corollary that the larger the organization, the longer the legal paperwork it generates. And one of the biggest offenders in terms of unnecessary length has become the social media policy.

First, a bit of history.

When blogs first emerged on the corporate communications landscape, employers really had nothing in place to help guide their employees on how to use the new medium. What emerged was sometimes embarrassing — inappropriate language, accidental (or not) disclosure of confidential information, and more.

Employers, acting in fear of the unknown, clamped down with rigid controls, asking workers to adhere to extremely tight policies — all posts needed to be reviewed by the legal team and include disclaimers at the bottom.

This all but shut down dialogue in the important social sphere, where an increasing number of people were turning to get news about companies. To this day, many large organizations have massive policies which serve more to keep communication down than to open it up.

A more human approach is to understand that people who are engaged and happy with their work want to talk about it, share news, and ask customers and stakeholders for their opinions. This should be encouraged.

TOUCH

This isn't to suggest that you don't need a strong policy. Indeed you do. It's just that it doesn't need to be burdened with legalese that frightens your team members into communications paralysis.

Creating a human social media policy doesn't come naturally. So, here are five simple steps you can take to strike the right balance between opening up communication and keeping internal things internal.

1. **Create a working group.** Involve people from all divisions of your organization — make sure you have representation from legal, communications and marketing, and senior management. And, include keeners who have a solid following on social networks.

2. **Create a trademark/copyright brief.** Much of the confusion and mistakes made on errant social media posts revolve around trademark, libel, and copyright issues. Prepare a human-language one-page brief about appropriate use of your intellectual property assets and those of your competitors.

3. **Use real-world examples.** People understand concrete examples better than abstract policies. Provide examples of excellent use of social channels both within and outside your organization, and highlight instances where a better approach could have been used.

4. **Encourage human language.** Encourage your employees to speak with an informal voice, in the way they would communicate with friends. Besides being easier to read, this tone makes it more likely people within their network will respond to and engage with your company news.

5. **Schedule annual policy reviews.** Social media changes constantly. Make sure you keep up with the times by assembling the working group at least every year to review

the latest communication channels available to people and to update your policy as required.

Of course, the best way to ensure that social media is used correctly is to hire the right people. During your hiring process, ask questions about how they'd promote company news within their own personal social networks. You might want to consider having them respond in essay form.

THE IP TRAP

If social media has done nothing else, it's given rise to the great Internet pile-ons of the digital era. There have been several examples of these involving intellectual property (IP) over the last little while.

One strong example of how not to respond to IP issues is what Ottawa photographer Barbara Cameron did. She kicked off an online hazing of local radio station Hot 89.9 and its parent company, Newcap Radio, for illegally using one of her photographs as part of a contest promotion. Photography website Shuttercliq published one of many blog posts written about the dispute. A counter-pile-on quickly erupted after the public became aware of a prior fraud conviction against Cameron.

Both sides mishandled themselves. However, Hot 89.9 was probably the bigger loser in the court of public opinion despite any support they may have had from the larger community. They made three critical mistakes which likely cost the station significantly more in wasted productivity than any amount they may have been required to pay in advance or as a negotiated settlement beyond the watchful public eye (including the reported two thousand dollars Cameron requested in an email exchange, which a Hot 89.9 respondent allegedly said was "extortion."). The radio station's mistakes were:

1. It was sloppy on their part to not source valid licensing before using the photograph in question. That move looked very uncommunity-like for a community-minded radio station.

241

2. They appeared to have dug in rather than try to come to a mutually-acceptable solution which could have worked to their advantage by turning an otherwise irate photographer into an accidental ambassador.

3. Even a week after the issue, they hadn't addressed the issue on their Facebook fan page, and they had disabled comments. Undeterred, the public took their anger to the recommendations section of the page.

Here are some key lessons from this experience.

1. Don't cut corners when it comes to intellectual property.

2. Mess up, fess up. Own the mistake and own the process of achieving a solution.

3. As hard as it may be, always be the better person. Digging in is adversarial. It will make you look bad eventually.

4. Finding a solution outside of the public eye is better PR. And it probably costs less.

5. If the problem is in the public domain, don't hide from it. Highlight your mistake (or publicly-perceived mistake) and what you are doing right now to correct it. Don't complicate the story with details people won't read.

ON THE HORIZON

Biometric Authentication Comes to Life

Inside the latest iPhones and iPads are secure fingerprint scanners. In the first release of this technology, though, the only function the scanners provided was unlocking the lock screen. In June 2014, Apple announced that its newest release of the mobile operating system iOS would permit developers to use this fingerprint authentication system in their own applications.

The impact of this development can't be overstated. Today's legal departments in organizations have access to digital signing capabilities (in the form of web services like HelloSign or EchoSign, or as simple signature imports in PDFs), though many companies have steered clear of these technologies because the chain of custody of the authentication can't be guaranteed — did the CEO really apply her signature to that contract, or was that her spouse at home dropping a digital graphic onto a PDF, trying to help out?

Expect to see Apple's technology, which is tied to a specific person, built out into a kind of "open touch" authentication standard, which will allow faster approvals on documents with stronger confirmation of the signer's true identity.

Emergence of the "Digital Shingle"

Lawyers no longer need to hang a wooden shingle outside their office to attract business. For years, attorneys have used digital marketing (to the extent permitted by their regulatory body, of course) like websites to promote their services. We're beginning, though, to see the natural extension of this shift — to lawyers doing their consulting work over secure web-conferencing systems.

Now that live video streaming isn't restricted to expensive tele-presence systems, some in the legal profession are finding that selling their time online by, literally, the minute, is a profitable venture indeed. Take the website *clarity.fm*, which describes itself as a "marketplace that connects entrepreneurs with top advisors and industry experts to conduct market research, get strategic business advice, or learn a specialized skill to help them grow their business." Lawyers and other professionals set a per-minute price and anyone can search for a specific area of expertise and buy just the amount of time they need for a quick consultation. Michael Cohen, CEO of Wrightwood Furniture, reports that "a $100 Clarity call stopped me from buying $30,000 in software that I didn't need."

A recent search of legal advisors on Clarity found most people charging between $1.50 and $5.00 per minute of consulting time.

Expertise ranged from a specialist in setting up franchise agreements to a music industry attorney to a technology patent researcher.

While this is a boon to individual lawyers, it could become a threat to retention of legal staff in your organization if this kind of technology really takes off.

TOUCHPOINTS: FIVE LEGAL TAKEAWAYS

 It's become a cultural phenomenon that people use technology to incorporate existing intellectual property into new creative works. This scares a lot of brands and lawyers. Remember, not every unauthorized use of your brand imagery demands legal action.

 Being heavy handed can backfire, resulting in bad press and possible online pile-ons. Finding solutions can get good press and earn credibility. Is winning a legal battle worth losing a brand war?

 People expect corporations to lead with legal muscle, even when dealing with individuals. Remember that people will be more willing to work with you if you treat them like people.

 Policies, contracts, cease-and-desist letters, and more, have become the domain of legal teams. What should be simple agreements now require law degrees to decipher. Speak a language people understand. There may be fewer legal disputes if you do.

 Individuals have remarkable power these days. And they're starting to figure that out. Work as a person with people, rather than against them. Solutions may come more quickly and be less costly.

CHAPTER 11
ANOTHER LETTER TO YOU FROM US

Dear Leader:

Mnemonic devices are powerful. They convey ideas and summarize procedures. The best mnemonics are portable — you can carry them with you wherever you go and save yourself the struggle of trying to remember the details

- The Heart and Stroke Foundation uses ABC (Alert, Breathing, Cardio) to help guide people through the process of delivering Cardio-pulmonary Resuscitation.

- To help students remember the correct order of mathematical operations, they are often taught "Please Excuse My Dear Aunt Sally" which guides them through operations starting with those embraced in Parentheses followed by Exponents, Multiplication, Division, Addition and finally Subtraction.

We hope that, as you continue to grow your organization, you keep TOUCH foremost in your mind. Think of it as five fingers on a hand — Technology, Outcomes, Uniqueness, Clarity, and Humanity.

Technology hasn't (fully) displaced humanity in the workplace, though it has distracted us from remembering we're human, as are those with whom we associate every day.

Thank you for reading our book. We wish you success as you embrace TOUCH. Please tell us how your progress toward TOUCH is going! Our direct email address is coauthors@touchthebook.com and our website is *http://touchthebook.com.*

Yours in humanity,

Tod and Mark

NOTES

1. Steve Jobs at the 1997 Apple Worldwide Developers Conference. Watch this video *www.youtube.com/watch?v=FF-tKLISfPE*

2. *www.youtube.com/watch?v=LJhG3HZ7b4o*

3. *www.youtube.com/watch?v=JGAL3m_uqUc*

4. *http://creativecommons.org*

5. *www.fastcompany.com/3001319/why-doing-awesome-work-means-making-yourself-vulnerable*

6. *www.ctvnews.ca/world/pope-francis-ignores-prepared-palm-sunday-homily-poses-for-selfies-1.1773757*

7. In Judaism, the cantor works closely with the rabbi to lead religious services. The cantor's role is generally more musical: the Paul McCartney to the synagogue's Ed Sullivan.

8. *www.youtube.com/user/PublicApologyCentral/videos*

9. *www.youtube.com/watch?v=SeQMMp4tXfk*

10. *www.youtube.com/watch?v=ZJxIHCbZmBw*

11. *www.youtube.com/watch?v=8LjUvYg5ysA*

12. *www.thestar.com/opinion/editorialopinion/2013/01/05/ without_school_sports_everyone_loses.html*

13. Statement from Chris Bolton, chair of TDSB:

    Oliver Moore and Simona Chiose, "TDSB Director Resigns over Plagiarism, PhD Dissertation Includes Unattributed Passages," *Globe and Mail*, January 10, 2013, accessed June 16, 2014, *www.theglobeandmail.com/ news/national/education/tdsb-director-resigns-over-plagiarism-phd-dissertation-includes-unattributed-passages/article7167752/?page=all.*

14. The hashtag #SMH is Twitter shorthand for "shaking my head."

15. The seemingly cryptic numbers of this tweet clearly mean bus number 4031 and route number 176

16. The jury is still out on whether or not this actually works with any systems, though the authors can attest they have tested this extensively over the years.

17. *www.youtube.com/watch?v=u2HD57z4F8E*

18. Yet.

19. Dunbar's number is the number of meaningful and stable social relationships one can manage at any given time, 150, as suggested by British anthropologist Robin Dunbar.

INDEX

ABOUT THE AUTHORS

Tod Maffin is president of engageQ Digital, a digital marketing firm specializing in creating human experiences for brands online. He speaks to more than forty conferences a year. He lives in Vancouver.

    Email: tod@engageQ.com
    Twitter: @todmaffin
    Website: www.todmaffin.com

Mark Blevis is president of FullDuplex.ca, a firm which specializes in integrated digital communication and online reputation management. He also heads a team that researches the role of online information and interactions in shaping public opinion. Mark lives in Ottawa.

    Email: mark.blevis@fullduplex.ca
    Twitter: @markblevis
    Website: www.markblevis.com